MARRIAGE:
For Better or for Worse?

MARRIAGE:
FOR BETTER
OR
FOR WORSE?

Robert H. Loeb, Jr.

A GROLIER COMPANY

FRANKLIN WATTS

New York/London/Toronto/Sydney/1980

Library of Congress Cataloging in Publication Data

Loeb, Robert H
Marriage.

Includes bibliographical references and index.
SUMMARY: Traces the origins and purpose of marriage,
discusses how changes in social structure have affected
family life, and examines marriage today in various
classes.
1. Marriage—Juvenile literature. 2. Teen-age
marriage—Juvenile literature. [1. Marriage] I. Title.
HQ734.L684   306.8   80–16403
ISBN 0–531–02879–8

CONTENTS

MARRIAGE:
For Better or for Worse?

FOREWORD

Fifty percent of those who come for psychiatric help do so because their chief problem is their marriage. Another twenty-five percent have serious marriage-related problems. Yet, the marital relationship has been the last to be studied by social scientists. This is partially due to the complexity and "private" nature of the marital relationship, but especially because it touches us all so closely and so deeply.

It is, therefore, particularly useful to have such a thorough, honest, and readable analysis of this most important relationship of adult life, next only in importance to that of the parent-child relationship of the early years. An ounce of prevention is worth a pound of cure, indeed.

Robert Loeb has achieved a remarkable synthesis of many crucial aspects of marriage—historical, sociological, and psychological. His selection of resource material is excellent, providing an introduction to important research, both current and in past decades. There are two refreshing aspects in this author's treatment of marriage. One is his exposition of the realistic impact of economic insecurity in blue-collar marriages: love does not conquer all. The other is his awareness of how the womens' movement places new stresses on men in the marital relationship. Yet he clearly recognizes the necessity for women to achieve equality.

Young people and their parents should profit from this sensitive and sensible exploration of the many reasons why marriages fail and what can make them work. Unlike many treatments of this emotionally charged subject, this one is not simplistic, nor is it romanticized or pessimistic. But it is written in a simple fluid style and should sustain the interest of the young adults and teen-agers to whom it is directed.

Adolescents, as well as their parents, can learn much of value as the engrossing subject matter sweeps them along from chapter to chapter.

Ida F. Davidoff, Ed.D.
Marital and Family Therapist
Associate Clinical Professor of Psychiatry (Counseling)
Emeritus, Albert Einstein College of Medicine

I
TWO BE OR NOT TWO BE?

Let me ask you a personal question: Do you expect to get married? The chances are ninety-nine out of a hundred that you will unhesitatingly answer yes. This affirmative reply is understandable and normal since 90 percent of Americans do eventually marry. And when I posed the question to high school students in several sections of the country, the answer was invariably yes.

But now let me ask you this: Do you expect to be happily married? Offhand this may seem to be an utterly ridiculous question. Who would enter matrimony with any other prospect in mind? The truth is, however, that it's a valid hope, but not a guarantee—in fact, far from it. Although most Americans jump on the marry-go-round, they only stay on it for a few whirls. Half of teen-age and early twenties marriages end in divorce, and the overall casualty rate for all marriages is one out of three. However, the marry-go-round keeps on whirling steadily because the majority of divorced people get back on for another ride and usually stay with it—for better or for worse.

But why not try to eliminate the risks of that first time

around? The way to accomplish this is to help you become aware of what marriage really is, stripped of its myths and mystique. When and why did it originate, where is it really at, and where is it going?

A number of social scientists (anthropologists, sociologists, and psychologists) maintain that the institution of marriage is in serious trouble. It is actually in a state of crisis, they say. The frequency of divorce attests to this. But this diagnosis is not, in itself, particularly helpful unless you understand why. And one of the chief reasons for today's marital fragility seems to be as simple as this: More is expected of marriage than ever before.

Why is that? Because of the drastic changes which have occurred in comparatively recent years in the structure of our society. History tells us that during 99 percent of mankind's existence, people depended on hunting and gathering (foraging for wild berries, roots, nuts, and greens) for survival. Then, in a relatively short period of time, we became a "modern" society. We choose to look upon this as "advanced, better," certainly no longer primitive. Unfortunately, the abrupt change from hundreds of thousands of years of "primitive" living to less than a hundred years of our "ultramodern" living is not necessarily a change for the better. As one social scientist evaluates it, "To date, the hunting way of life has been the most successful and persistent adaptation man has ever achieved." [1]

What has this got to do with marriage? The answer is both simple and quite complex. The simple factor is that the demands placed upon marriage in the hunting and gathering era were drastically different from those placed upon it today. Because our means of survival are so different, our life-style is different and our values are different. But our concepts of the purpose and functioning of marriage have not faced up to these basic changes.

Now for the complex aspects. Many of these are far from pleasant, but we must recognize them in order to cope with them. In the first place we must face up to the fact that the price we are paying for our so-called advanced civilization is not only high, but may be beyond affordability. Burgeoning industrial plants supply our insatiable cravings for more creature comforts, but they are polluting the air, water, and soil. This destructive side effect applies to our means of transportation by land and air. The ever-increasing demands for fuel to power our factories, cars, trucks, and planes have created an energy crisis. To "solve" this we have erected nuclear power plants. They, in turn, pose a constant threat to our survival. And our huge arsenal of nuclear weaponry, to which we keep adding over one thousand hydrogen bombs a year, threatens the extinction of the entire world. Although we don't wake up each morning and exclaim, "Oh my God, this may be our last day," these potentially lethal negatives tend to create an undercurrent of muted despair. And this, in turn, is bound to affect marital and family relationships as men and women face the future.

But, above all, it is the cataclysmic changeover from hunting and gathering to our superindustrial modern world that is endangering the viability of marriage. And this threat can only be overcome by becoming aware of what this has involved. Let's therefore explore some of the major factors of change.

The wife's role in the family

The wife's status is no longer solely dependent upon her capacity for reproduction, child rearing, and housework. Four-fifths of women today worked prior to marriage and 40 percent continue to work after marriage. Consequently a wife is no longer solely dependent upon a husband for economic support. Her growing independence has given her an awareness of her individual worth and also an awareness of male exploitation and domination in the past. Women's liberation has become a vital force. Although until recently it was restricted to upper socioeconomic, college-educated women, it has spread to the less advantaged as well. This enhanced sense of independence from the male and of self-worth has altered the wife-husband relationship. It has been abetted, as well, by woman's increased awareness of her right to sexual satisfaction as an equal in the partnership.

The husband's role in the family

Formerly, men married later in life. By the time their children reached maturity, the fathers were comparatively old men or often dead. In early days leisure time was at a minimum, except for the very wealthy. It was customary to work from dawn to dusk six days a week. There were no vacations, and annual holidays could be counted on two fingers. Because of this continual work load men scarcely had time to be sexually or emotionally restless or bored. Furthermore, they developed close ties to their working or business partners, whereas women relied on their female relations for emotional support. Thus husband-wife intimacy was more a matter of location—of living together—rather than an emotional bond.

People-to-people relationships

Today, lasting intimacy outside the home is a rarity. Our cities are too big and turbulent to foster it. The suburbs are in a continual state of flux, with families moving in and out. Our places of work do not encourage meaningful human relationships. White collar jobs are essentially impersonal, and blue collar, assembly line work assuredly so.

Conflicting value concepts

On the one hand, we bow our heads in reverence to the concepts of motherhood, love, unconditional commitment one to another—to mate and children. On the other hand, our heads snap to mesmerized attention to the words *achievement* and *prosperity,* which are based solely on financial success. Erich Fromm, the noted psychologist and social commentator, stated that we tend to *love things* and *use people* rather than the opposite. Social scientist Charles W. Hobart describes our conflict in values this way:

> This value confusion is, of course, a source of instability within the American family. A family presumes unlimited commitment between family members, "till death do you part" between husband and wife, "all we can do for the kids" on the part of parents toward children. But the priority of these love and concern values is directly challenged by success and achievement values which may imply that status symbols are more important than babies; that what a child *achieves* is more important than what he *is;* that what we *own* is more important than what we are.[2]

The foregoing are some of the major changes which are challenging the viability of marriage. With so many disruptive forces undermining it, why do people continue to marry at such an amazing rate? And why do six out of seven divorced people remarry? Furthermore, since living together is becoming increasingly common among young couples and among older people in the middle income group, why doesn't this trend make marriage obsolete?

The answer to each of these questions is the same and quite simple: People's essential needs for love, companionship, sexual gratification, self-reassurance, and escape from loneliness have not changed even though our social structure has done so abruptly. In fact, industrialization and consequent urbanization, though they have practically obliterated our traditional values, have not submerged these needs. If anything, the dehumanizing effects of mass production, mass consumption, and mass conformity (reinforced through our educational system and the mass media) have exacerbated the craving for these needs. Since they cannot be obtained at one's place of work or from the community, men and women seek love, companionship, compassion, and self-esteem from mar-

7

riage. In its millennia of existence, marriage was never confronted with such demands.

This then is the crux of today's marital fragility: demands which are difficult and sometimes impossible to satisfy. The resulting dissatisfactions cause divorce and then lead to the search for a new mate who the seeker hopes will meet these demands. The rise in marital infidelity does not deny the value of the marital state—probably quite the opposite, because in many instances husbands and wives seek outside sexual gratification in order to keep their marriage functioning. This may not always prove effective, but it demonstrates the desire of couples to stay married at any cost.

But why marriage, when couples can live together today, often without fear of social stigma? Why marriage, when we know that live-togethers can sustain each other's emotional needs without legal or ecclesiastical sanction? The answer seems to be that, despite the obvious fragility of marriage, despite whatever overt and covert cynicism exists, to date no viable substitute has been envisioned. There is a mystique about marriage rooted in tradition. But far more important and meaningful, getting married is a commitment, one to the other, and in the eyes of society. This applies despite the ease of obtaining a divorce. Thus there is no substitute for it despite its apparent tenuousness. As an interesting example, ". . . in one culture where the divorce rate approaches 100 percent, people still express the wish at every wedding that the marriage be a permanent one." [3]

The purpose of this book is to strip marriage of false concepts and put it in realistic perspective, minus myth and wishful thinking. We shall do this by tracing its origins and purpose from its inception. Next, we shall examine how the great changes in humankind's social structure affected family life. Then we shall look at marriage as it functions and malfunctions today for all classes of Americans. The majority of books on marriage are written about and for our affluent class. It, however, constitutes only 20 percent of our population. In order for you to be prepared for marriage, you should be well aware of how it affects everyone, rich and poor alike.

It is hoped that the end result of this panoramic view of marriage, its pros and cons, its fragility and strength, will encourage you to look carefully before you leap onto the marry-go-round. And perhaps you will decline the ride for a while, until you are more fully prepared. The more threatened and dehumanized our world becomes, the greater is our need for a loving, compassionate, supportive relationship, bonded by a sense of mutual commitment in order to avoid the pangs of loneliness and the ache of anomie. And marriage, despite its fragility, seems to offer the means to cope affirmatively.

SOURCE NOTES FOR CHAPTER I:

1. Arlene Skolnik, *The Intimate Environment* (Boston: Little Brown, 1978), p. 96.
2. Charles W. Hobart, *Commitment, Value Conflict and the Future of the American Family* (Cambridge: Schenkman Publishing Co., 1977), p. 29.
3. Skolnik, *The Intimate Environment,* p. 73.

II
ABOUT SAVAGES, MARRIAGE, AND MORALS

We stated in the previous chapter that marriage is not a modern invention, that it originated in prehistoric times. What was it and family structure like during the hunting and gathering stage of human history?

Much of what is "known" about those times is theoretical. But it is also based upon studies of people currently subsisting by hunting and gathering, and whose social patterns, it is assumed, closely resemble those of our prehistoric forebears. One of the prime things anthropologists want us to be aware of is that the simplicity of life-style in a hunting and gathering society does not imply living in a state of savagery. In religion, morality, art, and accepted patterns of behavior, their culture is, in its way, every bit as elaborate as ours.

Nor do anthropologists regard hunting and gathering people as being mentally inferior and having limited capacities for survival. In fact they find that they tend to be more relaxed sexually, for example, with premarital sexual freedom and no rigid condemnation of adultery. Although marriages are arranged by the elders, couples usually know each other first and have some freedom of choice in the selection of a mate.

13

And the element of love appears to be far more important in marriage than in agricultural and industrial societies.

Even more surprising, some anthropologists question whether our modern society offers as relaxed and abundant a way of life for husband and wife as do such "primitive" societies. A recent comparative study was made by a man-and-wife team of anthropologists. They spent over a year with a tribe of Peruvian Indians living in the Amazon rain forest. They compared the Machiguengas' way of life—essentially hunting and gathering—with that of "civilized, advanced," Frenchmen and -women.

This is what they found: (1) Frenchmen spend 24 percent more time working than Machiguenga men. (2) Frenchwomen (both housewives and working women) spend 20 percent more time working than Machiguenga women. (3) Frenchmen's time spent in consumption (this includes sports, travel, entertainment, eating, leisure, reading, school, and political activities) is triple that Machiguenga men. (4) Frenchwomen consume at four to five times the rate of Machiguenga women. The final tally is that Machiguenga men enjoy 40 percent more free time (sleep, rest, play, conversation, visiting) than Frenchmen and Machiguenga women have 50 percent more free time than Frenchwomen.

Professor Allen Johnson summarized his and his wife's conclusions as follows:

> It seems undeniable . . . that modern technological progress has not resulted in more free time for most people. . . . Increasing efficiency in production means that each individual must produce more goods per hour; increased productivity means, though it is not often mentioned, in this context, that to keep the system going we must consume more goods.[1]

Furthermore, more time is spent in care for our increasing number of possessions: cars, clothes, homes, boats, gadgets. Consequently, ". . . the increasing hectic pace of leisure activities detracts from our enjoyment of play, even when the increased stimulation they bring is taken into account." [2]

A further consequence, Professor Johnson states, is that we neglect many basic social needs because they are considered economically unproductive. These include care of the elderly and of children, egalitarian medical care, and other social aids.

I went into some detail with the foregoing study to eradicate, once and for all, the notion that our modern way of life is superior to that of the hunting and gathering era. Modern life seems to have a number of disadvantages which, in turn, directly affect the institution of marriage. However, there are a number of similarities in values and life-styles between then and now which disappeared with the advent of the agricultural period. Both marriage and sex practices in hunting and gathering societies seem to have resembled ours. In addition, the composition of the family was, like ours, *nuclear*—parents and children only, living under one roof. Their attitude toward child rearing resembled ours. They emphasized achievement, independence, and self-reliance, traits which modern parents encourage.

We have covered 99 percent of humankind's history in just a few pages. Now let's see what the changeover from hunting and gathering to an agricultural society and, subsequently, to an industrial society, did to marriage and family life, for what happened in the past has left its imprint on today.

The Agricultural Revolution

The agricultural revolution brought about radical changes in values and functions within the family and reduced women's status even further. Agriculture, as the means of survival, enabled people to settle down in one place. Property rights and the acquisition of possessions became paramount. This, in turn, brought about hereditary transmission, the passing on of land and other possessions from one generation to the next. The family structure changed from the nuclear to the ex-

15

tended patriarchal family. In contrast to the nuclear family, the extended family often included parents, children, plus immediate kinfolk and hired field hands, who all lived under the same roof.

In addition, there was a radical change of status within the family. The father became the omnipotent ruler of the household, and all females and younger members of both sexes were subject to his authority. Disciplined, hard work became the order of the day as contrasted to the comparatively leisurely routine of hunting and gathering people.

Respect, submission, and obedience from women and children to the father and to elder male relatives were mandatory behavior. This radically altered the wife-husband relationship and left its imprint deeply etched in twentieth-century agricultural societies. For example, in a study of peasant families in Roumania prior to Communist rule, husband-wife relationships were as follows: Unwritten laws required that a wife should not walk beside her husband, but follow behind him. At home she was to be his obedient servant to be beaten if she did not comply satisfactorily. In the fields she had to participate in some of the heaviest work alongside her husband, and even advanced pregnancy did not excuse her from these chores. Consequently, childbirth in the fields was a common occurrence.

In a recent study of agrarian peasant families in Teopoztlan, Mexico, the father's supreme status is clearly defined. He avoids all social intimacy with his family and sits alone, or with his grown sons only, at meals. His wife makes certain that the children are quiet so as not to disturb him. She is expected to teach them to fear their father, as she does.

The settling of New England in 1620, and for several decades after the American Revolution, serves as an excellent example of an agricultural society in flux. Although originally the majority were not of the Puritan faith, the English immigrants were ruled by the Puritan clergy. And the clergy clearly defined sexual and marital relationships in their agrarian economy.

However, many of us today have mistaken concepts of Puritan morality and attitudes toward sex. We associate Puritanism with regarding sexual conduct of any kind as an abomination of the devil. The court records and sermons of the time belie this completely. The Puritan clergy not only accepted the fact that men and even women had strong sexual drives, but encouraged them to give in to them *provided they were married*. Samuel Willard, a Puritan minister, wrote the most complete textbook on Puritan divinity. In it he frequently expressed his condemnation of "that Popish conceit of the Excellency of Virginity." John Cottton, another well-known clergyman, expressed his contempt for Platonic love.

In discussing marital sex, another minister stated that:

> "the Use of the Marriage Bed" is "founded in man's Nature," and that consequently any withdrawal from sexual intercourse upon the part of the husband or wife, "Denies all reliefe in Wedlock unto Human necessity: and sends it for supply unto Beastiality when God Gives not the gift of Continency." . . . These were the views of the New England clergy, the acknowledged leaders of the community, the most Puritanical of the Puritans.[3]

Ostensibly, the Puritans were most hostile to sexual intercourse outside marriage. Adultery was a capital offense, and fornication (mainly sexual relations between unmarried people) was punishable by whipping, being set in the stocks, or by branding. But, in actual practice, they did little more than frown upon such transgressions—and with good reason, since so many broke those laws.

Court records show that the great majority of crimes committed at that time involved adultery and fornication. Those cases were so numerous that the death penalty was only

17

carried out three times during a span of almost half a century. Instead, a man accused of adultery was made to stand on the gallows for an hour with a rope around his neck. Other punishments were whipping, sometimes branding, and/or a fine.

As is evident, the Puritans were aware that punitive measures of any kind did practically nothing to curb the lusty, libidinal drives of the people. Therefore they concluded that the only effective, sensible way to counteract fornication was to encourage marriage in every way possible. To accomplish this it had to be made as durable and attractive as possible. This feat was attempted in a number of interesting ways.

As one example, if a husband left his wife, but was still under a district's jurisdiction, he was compelled to return to her. Thus, when John Smith deserted his wife to live with Patience Rawlins, he was sent home minus ten pounds (his fine) and plus thirty stripes from a whipping. In another instance, Mary Drury left her husband on the grounds that he was impotent. The court, however, refused to believe her. She was fined five pounds and sent back to him.

The courts went further than trying to make certain that couples stayed together. They tried to make marriage a strife-free, enduring relationship. Husbands and wives were forbidden to strike each other. The law went even further to assure marital tranquility. As an example, and not an atypical one, a husband was ordered to post bond for good behavior because he had used "ill words calling her whore and cursing her." Conversely, Christopher Collins' wife was accused of railing at him, calling him "Gurley gutted divill." In this instance the court ruled that she had justifiable cause and acquitted her.

This last example might lead one to believe that the Puritans regarded men and women as equals. This was not so. A wife's position was patently inferior to a husband's as illustrated in this seventeenth-century record.

The dutie of the husband is to travel abroad to seeke living; and the wives dutie is to keepe the house. The

18

dutie of the husband is to get money and provisions: and the wives, not vainly to spend it. The dutie of the husband is to deale with many men: and of the wives, to talk with few. The dutie of the husband is, to be entermeddling: and of the wife, to be solitairie and withdrawne. The dutie of the man is, to be skilfull in talke: and of the wife, to boast of silence. The dutie of the husband is, to be giver: and of the wife, to be saver . . . Now where the husband and wife performeth the duties in their house we may call it College of Qyietness: the house wherein they are neglected we may term it hell.*4*

This attitude has carried through, in part, to today: husband, the provider, head of the household; and wife, the heart, hands, and feet, nurturer and provider of comfort and domestic service.

A study of seventeenth-century Andover, Massachusetts, records reveals attitudes toward marriage and family structure which affected these institutions for centuries. Andover was settled in the early 1640s. The marriage records of the second-generation settlers show that, as is the case today, women generally married at a younger age than men. Sixty-six out of seventy second-generation daughters married at an average age of 22.8 years.

The men married at an older age, the average for second generation sons being 27.1 years. And almost 25 percent married after they were 30. The reason for this surprisingly late age of marriage for men resulted from economic causes and the power of the patriarchal family setup (the father as supreme ruler). Fathers did not wish to part with their sons until the last possible moment because they needed them to help work the farm. They were a source of free labor. And when a son found a woman he wished to marry, he had no way to support her. Having earned nothing from his work on the family farm, he had to depend on the willingness and abil-

19

ity of his father to provide him with land on which he could build a house, plant crops, and raise cattle. Thus teen-age and early twenties marriages were a rarity. In turn, the young women had to sit by and wait until a male appeared who was in a position to propose marriage.

The long arm of father-power did not relinquish its grasp after a couple married. As a rule, when a father gave his son property, he held on to the deed. Consequently, the groom remained a dependent until his father died. And the average age of death for the original Andover settlers was 71.8 years of age.

From those early days to the beginning of the nineteenth century, there were no significant changes in the structure of family and marriage because agriculture was the chief means of survival for most people. The sole exception came with the rise of a mercantile and professional class in the cities. But in the towns and villages the tinsmiths, blacksmiths, potters, and shopkeepers depended upon farming as their chief form of livelihood. In other words, it was an agricultural society.

The Industrial Revolution

Then came the Industrial Revolution. It started, one might say, sneakily, in 1790 in Pawtucket, Rhode Island. But from the early 1800s on, it burgeoned into a force which cataclysmically changed the entire social structure of Americans. To start with, it took women, as well as children, out of the home. In the early 1800s, the majority of the workers in the spinning and weaving mills and factories were women and children.

This changed woman's status. She not only was outside the home, but contributed to family support. Now, instead of being exploited by her husband or father, she was exploited by the factory owners and their overseers. However, because she made an economic contribution to family support and because she worked alongside other women, she gradually became aware of her unjust subjugation by a male-dominated society. In fact, the first textile strike in New England, in 1824, included women who organized themselves independently.

In the second half of the nineteenth century, industrialization, in the eastern part of the United States, spread like a forest fire from one community to the next. Factories became larger and larger, manufacturing processes became more complex, and heavy industry came into being. Factory work consequently became more dangerous and arduous, and women and children were no longer deemed fit to be part of the work force. As a result, women were relegated to the home and became, once more, completely dependent upon men for survival.

The rapid growth of cities and the influx of people from rural to urban communities greatly affected the family structure as well. The extended family of the agricultural era reverted to the nuclear family of the hunting and gathering times. Thus modern industrial society started to resemble our earliest societies in a number of ways:

> The modern industrial society, with its small independent family, is then like the simpler hunting and gatherer societies . . . for some of the same reasons, namely limited need for family labor and physical mobility. The hunter is mobile because he pursues the game, the industrial worker, the job.[5]

With a cursory glimpse of prehistory, we took a quantum leap into what we term "modern times" with the coming of the Industrial Revolution and its impact on social structure in the mid-nineteenth century. It is hoped this has made you aware of the influences of the past on today's marital scene, for the present can be best understood by being aware of its roots.

In the next chapter we'll study the changes in family and marital structures from the mid-nineteenth century to the mid-twentieth century. You will see that the changes in concept and purpose of marriage accelerated at an almost overwhelming rate. And it is these drastic changes which you will have to cope with and understand as you face the prospect of matrimony.

SOURCE NOTES FOR CHAPTER II:

1. Allen Johnson, "In Search of the Affluent Society," *Human Nature,* September, 1978, p. 53.
2. Ibid, p. 55.
3. Edmund S. Morgan, "The Puritans and Sex," from *The American Family in Social Historical Perspective* (New York: St. Martin's Press, 1973), pp. 282–284.
4. Bernard J. Stern, "The Family and Cultural Change," from *Marriage Today* (Cambridge: Schenkman Publishing Co., 1977), p. 41.
5. Skolnik, *The Intimate Environment,* p. 111.

III
SEX AND MARRIAGE IN THE "GOOD OLD DAYS" OF YESTERDAY

Many older people, such as parents and especially grandparents, tend to look upon the comparatively recent past with nostalgia. They like to believe that in those "good old days," peace, love, and domestic tranquility were the rule. They believe that there was a far more solid relationship within families in those days; husbands, wives, and children respected each other, and there was none of today's rebelliousness, turbulence, and eroding doubts. On the other hand, most young people don't think about the recent past; they're concerned only with the *now*.

Both viewpoints are lacking in perspective. Years ago, attitudes toward marriage, morals, and sex were riddled with heinous concepts. The supposed solidity of relationships between wife and husband, and parents and children during those times is a myth, a cover-up which conceals the oppression of women especially. On the other hand, to disregard those times is equally foolish. They influenced your great grandparents' attitudes toward marriage, morals, and sex, which were passed on to your grandparents, who passed them on, in some instances, to your parents. Therefore to learn the realities of those times, particularly regarding marriage and women's role, will help to destroy the belief that today's morals and marriage are vastly inferior to then. Despite divorce, doubts, and frequent disillusionment, the change is for the better—especially for wives.

What was it like to be an American woman in the mid-nineteenth century? A study of women's magazines, religious and gift books published between 1820 and 1860, is quite revealing. Although the ideals expressed in those publications related to the goals and roles of middle- and upper-class women, they undoubtedly set equally impossible standards for all women. The author of this particular study sums up how a "true woman" of the times was to evaluate her worth and be judged by her husband and society: ". . . [it] could be divided into four cardinal virtues—piety, purity, submissiveness and domesticity. Put them all together and they spelled mother, daughter, sister, wife—woman." [1]

A woman's purity was on a par with her piety, and impurity was considered both unnatural and unfeminine. The magazines and religious tracts constantly warned that loss of her virtue, by *"allowing* herself to be seduced," invariably led to insanity. Fictional variations on this theme were popular in the women's magazines and seemed to promote the premise that a woman's psyche was in her hymen, not her brain.

These lines from a poem published in 1853 "eloquently" sum up the ideal American bride's attributes:

> "Her eye of light is the diamond,
> Her innocence the pearl,
> And these are ever the bridal gems
> That are worn by the American girl." [2]

What were this pure and lovely bride's duties as a wife? She was to be the leading light in matters of religious piety and purity of thought. She was also household domestic and nurse to the sick, for sickness, in those days, was a frequent occurrence. In addition, she was to be a comforter to her husband and sons so that they would not be tempted to look outside the home for female pampering.

Woman was assigned an additional activity to justify her existence: motherhood. This mandated role did not stop at bearing children. It also included rearing them in the paths of virtue, as father was too busy supporting the family to offer spiritual guidance.

These were the ideals which the literature of the nineteenth century reflected and propagandized. But, as time went on, some women started challenging such guidelines as unrealistically restrictive. Others felt guilty because they could not live up to them and searched for more comfortable alternatives. Change gradually came about. In the latter part of the nineteenth century the feminist movement started making ripples, then waves. In addition to fighting for the right of women to vote, the movement concerned itself with such issues as the right to work, the right to a college education, and for a change in women's dress. Liberating women rebelled against the tight corsets and hoop skirts and proposed wearing the less restrictive "bloomer" outfits consisting of pantaloons and tunics.

However, most of the women in the movement remained fettered to Victorian sexual standards. They accepted sexual intercourse as an unpleasant act which had to be tolerated for the sake of pleasing their husbands. And they felt that celibacy, for women, was not a deprivation but rather a "blessed relief."

By the beginning of the twentieth century, however, a strange statistical phenomenon relating to marital stability manifested itself. In 1880 there was one divorce for every twenty marriages. By 1900 there was one for every twelve marriages—a 40 percent increase. And by 1909 the ratio jumped to one divorce for every ten marriages. Thus in less than a generation and a half, the divorce rate had doubled.

Members of the clergy and religious zealots joined ranks

to combat this "satanic" trend but, despite their vehement efforts, to little avail. A liberating trend was already on its way. In England and on the Continent in the 1880s and 1890s, there were signs of protest against the indissolubility of marriage. Henrik Ibsen's plays *A Doll's House* and *Ghosts* had a strong impact on European audiences and, when seen here, on American audiences as well. In addition, a number of English intellectuals started attacking the bonds of Victorian marriage. H. G. Wells was among the protesters. He went so far as to predict the end of monogamy and restrictive sexual standards within a hundred years.

The American press started airing these revolutionary views, and the consequent publicity brought about affirmative results. Liberal-minded Americans in the upper socioeconomic class began to realize that traditional marriage was tyrannical and particularly repressive for wives. Oddly enough, though the feminists defended divorce, they did so not because it might permit women a more free sex life, but quite the opposite. It would protect women from the excessive sexual appetites of husbands and allow them the peace of celibacy.

By 1904 the profeminists and other liberals were given academic, professional endorsement. George E. Howard, historian and social scientist, stated that the rising divorce rate was having a salutory effect on America's social structure. Industrialization, urbanization, and other social stresses, he maintained, were breaking up the old patriarchal family concept, and this breakup was advantageous for all. This caused more divorces which in turn brought about a new kind of marriage which encompassed higher standards and permitted greater freedom for both marital partners.

His beliefs were subsequently endorsed and elaborated upon by other social scientists and, by 1910, even the conservative American magazines were publishing articles which at least acknowledged that there might just be two sides to the question of divorce. At this stage the moral conservatives realized that their cause was a losing battle. Their resignation allowed for further changes in attitudes toward morals, marriage, women, and divorce. These came to a head directly after World War I.

To help the men of the upper class, especially, cope with the situation and keep women in "their place," some clergymen and many doctors came to the rescue of *man*kind. One of the most influential, of the former, was the Reverend John Todd (1800–1873). Aside from his clerical duties he was a prodigious writer. Among his many books, *The Student's Manual* became a best seller upon publication and remained so throughout the nineteenth century. Unfortunately, this book cast its spell upon hundreds of thousands, if not millions, of young men and reflected the beliefs of the medical profession of the times.

Its chief assertion was that, to maximize the power of the mind, a man who wished to achieve success in the business world had to channel his energies to the mind and away from other parts of the body. And the worst sapper of a man's energies was sexual activity. In young men it was generally confined to masturbation. Since the discharge of sperm used up practically all of the energies, masturbation for young men was a prime evil. His popularization of this theory caused the belief in the evils of masturbation to become a national phobia. Despite physiological enlightenment, this belief is still held by some today.

However, the mandate for a man to avoid sexual activities was not confined to masturbation. The medical profession counseled husbands and wives to keep the male's sperm souped up, so to speak, to a maximum level of richness. Thus it was to be used solely for the purpose of procreation and not for pleasure. And it is here where women became the real victims of the spermatic-economy theory. Gynecologists asserted that women were governed by their generative organs. And because they were the sperm absorbers they sapped men's energies. In other words, the female was a threat to the male.

The phobia about woman's male-sapping sexual drives

caused hideous, medical counteraction in the latter part of the nineteenth and early part of the twentieth centuries. Doctors asserted that women's proclivities toward masturbation infused them with boundless sexual cravings. In order to "cure" this, American gynecologists put their trusty scalpels to use. From about 1867 right through to 1904 and possibly as late as 1924, clitoridectomy was widely performed. It involved the removal of the entire clitoris, a procedure which was castigated by British doctors.

A "milder" procedure even more widely practiced—and only in the United States—was to circumcize girls and adult women. It consisted in cutting away a piece of skin, the "hood," above the clitoris. The scalpel wielders maintained that this curbed woman's desire for masturbation and her unappeasable sexual appetite caused by unsatisfactory intercourse.

Climaxing the drive to reduce women to a minimum of viability was the introduction of female castration. This horror was invented by a Southern surgeon, Robert Battey of Rome, Georgia. He claimed that removal of the ovaries cured female neurosis, insanity, abnormal menstruation, and practically all other disruptive symptoms indigenous to the female. The latter included being troublesome, overeating, attempted suicide, erotic tendencies, and, of course, masturbation.

Battey's "cure" caught on with a vengeance beyond belief. Women were castrated by the hundreds of thousands, from North to South, from the East to the West Coast. By 1890, and continuing on its maiming way until at least 1921, it was a thriving industry for American gynecologists.

These maiming practices were mainly confined to women in the upper economic class since only they, or their husbands, could afford them. Their willingness to undergo these procedures seemed to be based on hopeful resignation.

After World War I, a drastic change occurred in the status and especially in the attitudes of women in the upper middle class. By the 1920s the flapper appeared upon the scene, a rebellious woman with bobbed hair, powdered nose, short skirt, holding a cigarette and accompanied by a man, *not* necessarily her husband. Smoking, drinking, jazz, "flaming youth," and petting became the rage. Although remote to the working classes, the liberated sensuality represented by the flapper had some effect on them. Among middle-class women the incidence of premarital intercourse rose sharply and sexual equality became at least a debatable subject.

But then came the Great Depression of the thirties. One out of four men became unemployed, and the remainder were in constant dread of losing their jobs. The male breadwinner once again became the paramount family figure. Women in the labor force were castigated for taking jobs away from men. Consequently, the inchoate women's revolution of the twenties was repressed by the overwhelming forces of depression times.

However, World War II came to the rescue of America's economic plight. Manufacturing plants whirred with activity, making their contribution to "the war effort" and to corporate profit. The need for manpower allowed womanpower to participate. Even children, three and a half million of them aged fourteen to seventeen, were permitted the dubious privilege of contributing to the corporate tills by working in factories. Over thirteen million men were in the armed services. Even women were allowed to do their military bit—womanly things, to be sure—by enlisting in the WACS and the WAVES.

One might think that this dramatic change in social structure would have caused a complete change in attitudes toward marriage, family, and woman's status—but it didn't. Because, with the end of the war, men were back in the job market and the government wanted women to return where they belonged: to the home. Social scientists, the mass media, and so-called liberal groups joined forces to get women back to assuming their "proper" functions, as mothers and household domestics.

The emphasis on motherhood and domesticity resulted in the "baby boom" of the late forties and early fifties. Thus we have now reached the threshold of today, for it was this baby boom generation, your parents, who have directly influenced the family and marital climate you are facing. And it is the sum total of what transpired in the late nineteenth and earlier twentieth centuries which has shaped the matrix for today's matrimony.

SOURCE NOTES FOR CHAPTER III:

1. Barbara Welter, "The Cult of True Womanhood in 1820–1860," from *The American Family in Social-Historical Perspective* (New York: St. Martin's Press, 1973), p. 225.
2. *The Young Lady's Offering: or Gems of Prose and Poetry* (Boston, 1853), p. 283.

IV
AMERICAN MYTHS
AND MARITAL REALITIES

Despite the closeness of the 1950s and early 1960s, those days have been obscured by a fog of myths about American family life and marriage. And obviously, where marriage is at today is immediately related to yesterday. Therefore it's important to be aware of the reality, rather than of the mythology.

In the fifties and sixties there seemed to be a perpetual economic boom as well as a baby boom. It looked as if every man, woman, and child in America could and did enjoy a generous slice of the country's continually growing gross national product. This, however, was far from the truth.

It was also believed that the head of the typical American family, Dad, joyously commuted to his reward—his corporate job in the city—and spent his weekends in happy family togetherness. The family that prayed together, played together, and shopped together—stayed together. And Mom, too, was delighted with her role. She loved being a housewife and homebody. She reveled in being the "perfect" parent to her brood of three to five children. The mass media, especially the women's magazines, propagandized the myth that American women wanted above all to get married, have many children, and find

35

fulfillment in child rearing, gourmet cooking, and beautifying their homes.

The same media also promoted the myth that all American males enjoyed upward mobility and economic security. In short the belief was broadcast, via print, TV, and radio, that the U.S.A. had finally achieved the divine destiny of a capitalist society: health, wealth, security, and happiness for all regardless of race, color, sex, or creed.

How nice it would have been, and continue to be, if all of this were a reality, because economic security, good health, and minimum outside tensions promote marital contentment. Unfortunately, it was and is far from the truth. Some of the unpleasant realities started being aired in the early sixties. The "surprising" discovery was made that there were over twenty million Americans living under deplorable conditions: undernourished, poorly housed, and medically and educationally deprived. A large proportion were blacks, both in the South and in the inner cities of the North.

But there was an additional large percentage of Americans who, though not that deprived, did not live in the lap of middle-class luxury. These were the blue-collar workers and their families.

Then another disturbing reality destroyed the myth of the blissfully happy, middle-class housewife. Feminists started making women aware of the ways in which they had been, and continued to be, exploited and discriminated against in both business and in the professions and that being relegated to the role of housewife and child rearer was a form of marital exploitation.

The end of "the American dream" began with the realization that men in the middle and upper income groups were not all frolicking and romping in green pastures of guaranteed upward mobility and job security. In the late sixties the American economy started to falter. A recession set in and eroded the notion of "the affluent society." It also eroded the myth of job security and guaranteed upward mobility for middle-class males. It became obvious that these men had rarely been the joyful, contented husbands, fathers, and breadwinners they had been pictured to be. Job insecurity, fear of employment obsolescence due to aging, and corporate politics disturbed their emotional equilibrium. The depersonalizing ambiance of the corporate structure caused a number of them to question their workaday purpose.

In addition, the inroads of feminism caused these men to fret about their role in the family, in the marriage, and even in the bedroom. Analysts' couches were kept at body temperature from the continuous procession of supine bodies of the executive class seeking help.

You may wonder why extraneous subjects such as work, income, housing, health, etc., are discussed in a book about marriage. The reason is that each and all of these social phenomena directly affect marriage and family relations. Negative stresses create tensions and discord. Therefore, let's briefly examine the social realities of today.

Unemployment has become a way of life for at least 6 to 8 percent of the working class. One out of five blacks and other minority people are jobless (20 percent), and 40 percent of young men and women in their teens face unemployment. Inflation is gnawing away at the incomes of the majority of Americans. This is causing some of yesterday's necessities— such as adequate housing, good dental and medical care—to be today's luxuries for too many. In addition, everyone is facing an eroding ecology and an energy crisis.

The sum total of such negative stresses directly affects the institution of marriage and family structure. An ambiance of threat, impermanence, and frustration is bound to have corrosive side effects on human relations. And that is what marriage involves above all else. It also has caused a drastic change in Americans' social values. These, in turn, are bound to make the purpose of marriage and the relation between husband and wife, and between parents and children, different.

One example: The Protestant work ethic was pervasive

for centuries. Its rubrics were self-denial, foregoing immediate self-gratification for future security, work for work's sake. Today there is a new attitude, a polar opposite. One social commentator has dubbed it "pop-hedonism," another, "the culture of narcissism." It manifests itself in a way of life based upon display, play, fun, and spending as the goal. It involves the instant gratification of *self,* and advocates self-fulfillment through self-awareness at the expense of other-awareness. It's me, myself, and I, with the *I's* having the overwhelming votes over the *you's.* Religious cults and group therapy schools purport to raise one's consciousness level in order to attain new levels of awareness, devoted invariably and exclusively to *self.* It's obvious that putting one's self first is bound to create changes in marital attitudes.

The women's movement, too, is changing many formerly cherished values. With more and more women in the labor force and the professions, the submissive, economically dependent female is ceasing to be woman's role. The movement's drive for sexual equality is not only casting the traditional male's role adrift from its macho mooring, it is also causing fission within the concept of the nuclear family.

The combined effects of these value changes alone mean that ". . . the family is different than it was in the past, the society it inhabits is different, and Americans as individuals are different." [1] It is this that one must keep in mind: that marriage and family structure are undergoing change in order to adapt to the changes in our total social structure. Our present high divorce rate and the greater demands made upon marriage are due to these shifting values. The prognosis for the world's future viability may be clouded with doubt, but we must continue trying to make the best of the given conditions and cope with them in a positive way. This involves facing up to the realities of matrimony rather than the myths. What do they include?

American women, regardless of socioeconomic class, derive fewer advantages from marriage than men. Stated bluntly, marriage is often disadvantageous to them whereas it is beneficial to men. Studies indicate that married men are far better off mentally and physically than those who remain single. After middle age, married men's physical health is better than that of men who have never married. Regardless of age, married men enjoy better mental health and far fewer psychological distress symptoms than single men. The suicide rate of the latter is double that of married males. The price married men pay for their greater longevity and emotional stability is economic responsibility (having to support a family) and sexual restriction (monogamy).

But an increasing number of wives are sharing the burden of family support, and extramarital sex is not only becoming more commonplace, but increasingly socially acceptable. These trends tend to alleviate the two drawbacks many married men object to in marriage: economic responsibility and sexual restrictions. And if these trends continue, men can look forward to having their wedding cake and eating it, too. They can enjoy the love, companionship, economic aid, and sexual availability provided by their wives, and they can indulge in extramarital sex as well.

What about married women? Numerous studies show that more wives than husbands consider their marriages unhappy, have considered separation or divorce, and have regretted being married. Even among happily married couples, wives report twice as many areas of dissatisfaction as husbands. These include finances, religion, sex, friends, and life goals. While the physical health of wives is on a par with husbands, studies indicate that they suffer more mental health problems such as phobic reactions and states of depression.

Does this mean that women are born more psychologically fragile than men? The answer is no. A study made in the late 1930s, when single women were looked upon with suspicion and disdain, showed that, despite their inferior social status, they suffered from fewer emotional discomforts than married women. Recent statistics reveal that emotional prob-

39

lems are more frequent among married than single women. What are some of the stresses which seem to impair married women's emotional health? What are some of the social forces which restrict a wife's potential to continue developing as an individual, to enjoy a sense of fulfillment?

1. *Loss of status upon marriage.* In the eyes of society a woman achieves her destined role when she becomes a wife. Nevertheless, it is also looked upon as a step down, not a step up, because traditionally a wife's status becomes inferior to her husband's. She is assigned the number two position, he, number one.

2. *Loss of legal status.* Adding to this second class role is the fact that, in a number of states, a wife's legal status is inferior to her husband's and to a single woman's.

3. *The trauma of betrayal.* The majority of women are still reared to believe that they are "the weaker sex" and that they will be protected and comforted by "the strong, confident male." But upon marriage they quickly discover that a husband is not all man but *human* and thus subject to human frailties. He often is at a loss to solve his own problems, let alone his wife's. Consequently she discovers that he, not she, is the one who needs comforting—a switch in roles for which she may have been unprepared.

4. *The end of romantic trappings.* During the courtship period her future husband is on his best behavior and goes out of his way to cater to her. But after marriage she is expected to do the catering instead.

5. *Having to accommodate herself to her husband.* Despite increasing enlightenment as to male-female roles, it still is an unwritten law that a wife should tailor her life-style to her husband's wishes, work, and habit patterns. Studies show that wives make many more of the adjustments called for in marriage than husbands. This unfair need for accommodation is abetted by most marriage counselors and other therapists. Far too frequently they suggest that the wife make proper adjustments to keep the marriage going. This attitude results in

stunting a married woman's personal development and self-esteem during the early and middle years of her marriage.

6. *Abrupt change in occupation.* Despite the frequent possibility that a bride may have a job, she often starts off her marriage by becoming a housewife—for some, a euphemism for "domestic servant"—a job which she did not necessarily choose of her own free will. In many instances it has serious consequences. One author describes this dilemma as follows:

> . . . By comparing married housewives with married working women, we find that wives who are rescued from the isolation of the household by outside employment show up very well. They may be neurotic, but they are less likely than full-time housewives to be psychotic. In nearly all symptoms of psychological distress—from headaches to heart palpitations—the working women are overwhelmingly better off.[2]

Although marriage appears to be far more rewarding for husbands than wives, both face many of the same social stresses regardless of socioeconomic class. Briefly described they are as follows:

1. *Sexual adjustment.* Despite the sexual revolution, sexual maladjustments remain a paramount problem for married people. The sex-loaded messages of X-rated movies and sex-oriented TV and print advertising which bombard both children and adults, do not contribute to sexual enlightenment. If anything, they do quite the contrary. Positive sexual awareness among young adults in their mid- and latter teens is woefully lacking. In part this is due to their parents, the great majority of whose attitudes toward sex are anchored to the restrictions of the past.

As a child develops toward adulthood and its sexual drives can no longer be disregarded, parents often feel completely incapable and embarrassed to offer constructive sexual guidance. Compounding this smog of ignorance, sex education in the schools remains inadequate or does not even

41

exist. Thus by the time young people graduate from high school, or leave prior to that, they are generally sex-innocents when confronting heterosexual relationships and marriage. This does not mean that they may not have had sexual relations. They may know different ways to "do it," but this is limited to a physical act—more of an athletic contest with winner and loser. It's copulation qua copulation and robbed of any deep emotional interplay. Young people who go to college are more exposed to heterosexual relationships and sexual sophistication. Unisex dormitories are becoming increasingly common. Nevertheless after marriage, and even before, many of them flock to analysts, therapists, or marriage counselors, hoping to resolve their sexual problems. Thus they, too, have not escaped the effects of their childhood sexual ignorance.

2. *Economic stresses.* These stresses vary in degree and kind. Low-income families' problems involve providing food, clothing, and shelter. For the upper-income families they involve acquiring an endless list of "necessary" luxuries. Both groups face an identical problem: which comes first, job, or husband-wife and family relationships. For the less privileged, the blue-collar workers, the job must take precedence for the sake of survival. When there's a plant shutdown the worker must hunt in another locale for employment. The white-collar wage earners suffer similar uprootings. Corporations frequently move executives from one community to another. Such moves require continual adaptation to the new environment and are a source of familial stress.

3. *Health stresses.* Poor health, whether mental or physical, is a very disruptive factor in marital and family relationships, particularly among the middle- and low-income groups.

4. *Women's liberation.* The women's movement has been and continues to offer a significant, positive contribution to our society. The American woman has become increasingly aware that her rights extend far beyond equality in the job market. They include her right to self-development within the

marital structure; to making housework what it should be—a shared chore along with child rearing. They encompass her right to opt for a career in lieu of motherhood, her right to be on an egalitarian footing in all family functions, sexual, social, parental, and economic.

This requisite, though belated, balancing of the matrimonial scale, however, is requiring a good deal of readjustment on the part of husbands. Readjustment generally involves temporary stress. A husband must learn to adapt to his new role in marriage: as an equal rather than as a superior member of the partnership. His ego may shrivel and his libido may suffer from withdrawal symptoms for a period of time. Social progress—change—usually results in temporary disruption prior to adaptation.

This has been a brief overview of some of the basic realities involved in marriage which are shared by all classes. Our next chapter explores the specific problems faced by the economically and educationally more privileged.

SOURCE NOTES FOR CHAPTER IV:

1. Skolnik, *The Intimate Environment,* p. 5.
2. Jessie Bernard, "Marriage: His and Hers," from *Marriage Today: Challenge and Choice* (Cambridge: Schenkman Publishing Co., 1977), pp. 262–263.

V
MARRIAGE AND THE MIDDLE CLASS

What entitles one to be a member of the middle class? Money. In 1978, according to the Bureau of Labor Statistics, an income of $25,202 allowed for a "higher level" standard of living and an income of $17,106 just got an urban family into the middle-class bracket. Based upon these figures, how many middle-class families are there? Only 20 percent of American families fit the bill.

Why and whom do middle-class people marry, and what are the more common social pressures they face prior to marriage? Although some of the following answers apply to the lower-income groups, they apply particularly to the middle class:

Pressure to marry within one's class

There is a growing trend to evaluate individuals on their own worth regardless of their religious, racial, economic, or ethnic origins. Going hand in hand with this enlightened viewpoint is the belief that an individual is entitled to choose a companion, lover, and/or marital partner based upon his or her personal values. However, the forces of tradition remain all too powerful. Consequently, many young men and women are pressured to date, to live with, and to marry within their ascribed social status. And those who defy such assigned restrictions often face conflicts and confusion. These include criticism and even ostracism from parents because "she married beneath her class," or because "he married someone of another faith." These issues and how to cope with them are covered in a subsequent chapter.

External forces restricting or limiting partner selection

In choosing a marriage partner it would seem both logical and natural that the sole people involved in the selection should be she and he. However, this is an oversimplification and overlooks some basic realities which must be recognized. They are the realities of being and surviving, such as economic dependence on parents, relative intelligence levels, and emotional stability. If disregarded, any one of these issues can create problems at the very outset of the marriage. Therefore, the question that has to be faced is this: Are a man and woman who are in love and intend to marry, capable of objectively evaluating their suitability for one another? Quite possibly not. Should they, instead, rely on the judgment of parents, relatives, intimate friends, or professionals? Some marital experts believe that couples who rely solely on their own judgment are likely to meet with marital unhappiness. Others do not agree with this prognosis. This leaves the problem in limbo. There doesn't seem to be a simple, guaranteed solution.

Sex-role stereotyping

The word is spreading, though not fast enough, that we are programmed by parents and society to behave in strictly assigned artificial role patterns depending upon our biologically assigned sex. A male must act in a masculine fashion and a female in a feminine way. There is a growing awareness, however, that to behave in a "manly" fashion, or a "womanly" one, is nurture-, not nature-imposed. This more enlightened

48

viewpoint is not widespread as yet, and the majority of both sexes are still tethered to sexist beliefs. Thus a "real he-man" should conceal his emotions. He should be brave, aggressive, and assertive both in the marketplace and in his heterosexual relations. A "real she-woman" should be emotional, passive, and noncompetitive whether in the bedroom, the classroom, or the office. For her to act otherwise makes her suspect and "unfeminine."

More women than men are beginning to recognize that these are sex-stereotyped roles which have been far more limiting to the female than to the male. However, the liberated woman often finds that if she reveals that she is sexually aroused by her date's overtures, or if she makes the overtures, he is apt to label her a whore, because, if he's not equally enlightened, he may believe it's "natural" for him to be the sexual aggressor and "unnatural" for her. On the other hand, when a man recognizes the equality of the sexes and maintains that his date should share entertainment expenses, since she also works, she may find this unfair and resent it. Thus, until young men and women become equally and more fully aware of the malaise of sex stereotyping, confusion and conflict will continue to impede a sound relationship.

Love's enigma

"Love" is probably the most misunderstood word in our vocabulary. At best it's difficult to define. At worst it is used as an excuse for heedless, precipitous actions. Particularly in our American culture, love is supposed to be the primary basis for mate selection. However, the expression "I've *fallen* in love" too often describes the realistic position in which love has placed its "victim." He, or she, has fallen into a trap. The emotional highs, especially in the early stages of a heterosexual relationship, impede rational evaluations of the important factors involving the two. A common result is that marriages ensue too soon, and such matings are quickly beset with unforseen misunderstandings and resulting conflicts. For example,

49

was their love based solely on physical attraction and instantaneous sexual gratification? Or did it include, or arise from, a sense of shared commitment and companionship? One without the other does not engender a lasting, satisfactory liaison. Therefore, to avoid "falling in love," one should try to evaluate one's "being in love" in as rational a manner as is possible.

The fear of losing one's self

I pointed out that there is a rapidly growing trend toward self-gratification, toward "me-firstness." Consequently, the fear of losing or surrendering one's self, one's identity, in an emotionally charged heterosexual relationship looms as a potential hazard. Where does one draw the line between self and other? When does accommodation stop and surrender start? How does one maintain one's individuality and at the same time make the necessary compromises to mesh with the other's individuality? A durable, loving relationship requires a certain degree of self-surrender, and it definitely does not allow for a me-first attitude.

Those are some of the problems which young, middle-class people face prior to marriage. However, something else has loomed on the heterosexual horizon. More and more middle-class couples are living together prior to marriage and, although most of them eventually marry, they do not necessarily marry each other. Living together is becoming increasingly common among college students.

But even among this educationally advantaged group, sex-role stereotyping remains a negative force. Recent studies of their views about marriage and desired roles of husbands and wives confirm this. Thus 24 percent of the male students polled firmly stated that, ". . . they intended to marry women who would find sufficient fulfillment in domestic, civic, and cultural pursuits without ever seeking outside jobs."[1] Only 16 percent gave halfhearted approval to working wives, but under such restrictive conditions that their affirmative responses were, to all intents and purposes, negated. The balance (48 percent) approved of wives working, provided, however, that their basic responsibilities toward their children were not neglected.

One of the male students exemplified the predominant attitude:

> I would not want to marry a woman whose only goal is to become a housewife. . . . I don't think a girl [sic] has much imagination if she just wants to settle down and raise a family from the very beginning. . . . However, when we both agree to have children, my wife must be the one to raise them. She'll have to forfeit her freedom for the children.[2]

Since the great majority of young men and women of the middle class attend college, their desires and expectations from marriage and mates are more the rule than the exception. Where does this leave middle-class marriage today, and what are some of its most striking features?

An increasing number of middle-class wives are working, but this applies to the marginal members of this class. It is due more to necessity than a desire for independence and fulfillment outside the home. Inflation, regressive taxation, and consequent soaring costs of living make it mandatory for both wife and husband to work in order to maintain middle-income status. However, among the wealthier members of this class, the old values and traditions of husband-wife roles continue to exert a strong influence.

Thus the upper-income husband is apt to measure his worth as a person, and especially as a man, by being able to say: "My wife doesn't have to work." This attitude relegates the wife to the home. Whether it be a ten-room, custom-designed contemporary in exclusive suburbia, or on the twentieth floor of a security-guarded luxury apartment in the city, she is confined to her nuclear cell. She tends to judge her worth by her husband's success in the professional or corporate world. Thus her self-evaluation is achieved vicariously: by her husband's earnings and title and also through her children's success in school. A poll taken a few years ago asked middle-class women to list, in order of importance, the roles of their spouses. They placed breadwinner first, father second, and husband almost as an afterthought.

Where does this leave the breadwinner, Dad? Not in the driver's seat either at work or at home. At his office, unless he's chairman of the board, or chief stockholder of the corporation, there's a hierarchy of officials whom he must please and placate. His executive peers are more likely to be rivals whom he must be wary of, rather than friends. Furthermore, the large corporate structure, though it does not demand poverty or chastity, demands obedience—the submerging of self for the good of the company. Consequently, in order to rise, let alone survive, an up-and-coming executive must be an in-fighter encased in the armor of emotionlessness.

But when he returns home to his wife and children, he is supposed to be transformed into a playful, loving, feeling, carefree person. Understandably, it is almost impossible for him to make this transition, to forget the pressures and frustrations of his work the moment he crosses the threshold of his nuclear nest. Most of his energies, his ego involvement, and his time have been expended at his job. Consequently, he is more often "shell" than "self." To instantly join in play and relaxation with his family—not to mention coping with the natural demands of his wife and children—is difficult. Alcohol and other drugs, including tranquilizers, may temporarily ease the transition from one personality to the other. But this "cure" is more insidious than the "disease."

His problems at home do not end there. Today many women are aware that sexual satisfaction is not solely a man's prerogative. A woman can be both the initiator and take an active part in the pleasurable results of coitus. But despite their wives' various academic degrees, many success-driven males refuse to regard marriage as a partnership. They've been programmed to be domineering and aggressive. Thus their wive's sexual expectations pose a grave threat to their masculinity, their custom-tailored macho image. The constant competition they encounter in the business world is now carried into the bedroom. There they once again feel placed in a competitive situation. Result: ignominious retreat to pseudo-sexual passivity which can even manifest itself in impotence.

I have depicted a grim and generalized picture of middle- and upper-income marriages. In actuality the problems vary in degree, from acute to tolerable to benign. Nevertheless, the preceding describes what many up-and-coming, as well as downhill-and-going, members of the middle class face.

The myriads of books on marriage, written for and about the middle class, are filled with case histories. They serve as firsthand accounts of the problems which many of those men and women face. Let's take a look at a few of them.

The Greens. Henry, aged thirty-two, and Joan, thirty, had been married seven years. They had a son of five and a daughter aged two. They went to a psychiatrist hoping to resolve their deteriorating relationship. At their first session with the therapist, Henry said their problems amounted to: "Too much bitterness, little mutual satisfaction, and we continually fight about trivia."

Joan: "I wanted a strong husband, but not too strong or I would not be free. But Henry is more stubborn than strong. I can't play with him, and sex is poor. It's not frequent and I don't have orgasms anymore. And we don't even have sex unless I initiate it."

Henry was an engineer. He recently switched jobs because he preferred being in direct command of a large number of employees out in the field to being chained to paper work in an office. But the new position paid only two-thirds as much as the previous one. His wife was sympathetic, but she also wanted to maintain their high standard of living. This necessitated their having to accept money from her wealthy mother, or Joan's going to work for her mother, who

53

owned a successful business. But Joan's field was music, and she felt that joining her mother's business was contrary to what she wished to do. She complained that Henry did not sufficiently share in housework, nor in tending the children. But, above all, she felt that a man who did not make enough money for his family and expected his wife to help maintain their standard of living was weak.

However, Henry felt that he did give her the security and freedom from material concerns she desired. "I do give her that, but it's the damn money. I won't maintain our standard of living by doing work I dislike."

Whether and how this couple resolved their problems, though important for them, is irrelevant to our text. What is relevant is that they illustrate two of the middle-class marriage problems we discussed: the inexorable drive for conspicuous consumption and the conflict caused by a sexually liberated woman's demands in the bedroom.

The Hendersons. Pam and Ken Henderson sought psychiatric help after they had been married four years. He was twenty-nine and she twenty-seven. They had a child of two with another on the way. Prior to their marriage Pam had had a successful career. She had had her own home, traveled extensively, had numerous friends, enjoyed sex, and felt herself to be a liberated woman. Marriage made her feel that she had given up her freedom. A little over a year after their marriage, their relationship was in trouble. They had difficulty communicating with each other, and he suffered periods of depression without knowing why. At that time Ken sought therapy and became aware that he felt he was failing at his job and did not have the drive to make it to the top in the large corporation he worked for. He had always believed, however, that he would be a big success and could become part of the power structure of the business world. He resigned and took a job with a smaller corporation in another state.

Prior to the move, Pam had not been able to find suitable work in her profession. Her new suburban environment, plus her newborn baby, made her feel more trapped than ever. When they consulted the psychiatrist together, Ken said: "I understand Pam's need to work, her distaste of being enslaved to the home. But she knows she'll be sprung, so to speak, after the baby is born. But she knew we were tight for money and yet wanted children. Of course I know she wants to get out, and I want to make it possible for her to work because she isn't happy this way. But, I'm trapped, too, working twelve hours a day, six days a week right now. That won't last for too long, but for me to get ahead, that's the way it has to be right now. I don't want to split with her. We've had a rough time what with the change of jobs, less money coming in, and two changes in living areas in four years—plus one baby and another coming."

This case literally and figuratively speaks for itself. It dramatically portrays a number of problems facing middle-class couples which we discussed both statistically and in the abstract.

Now let's see what mate selection and marriage is like for the majority of Americans: the blue-collar workers, lower-income wage earners, and blacks.

SOURCE NOTES FOR CHAPTER V:

1. Joan Huber, ed., "Cultural Contradictions and Sex Roles," from *Changing Women in a Changing Society* (University of Chicago Press, 1973), p. 117. From article by Mirra Komarovsky.
2. Ibid., p. 120.

VI
MARRIAGE AND
THE WORKING CLASS

What "entitles" one to be a member of the working class? Generally, lack of money, lack of opportunity, lack of education, and often, the wrong color skin: black or brown.

Why are we devoting so many pages to working-class marriage, a subject which almost all books neglect? For two cogent reasons. One, the working class constitutes 80 percent of our citizenry. Two, they experience more marital problems and a greater incidence of divorce than do middle-class couples. And the underlying reasons for this marital instability are vital for you to understand so that you can avoid similar problems, or, at least, know what you may be in for.

Men in the middle- and upper-income classes work, too. They may start off with limited wage and job status, but, over a period of time, their positions in the professional or corporate world reach higher salary and title levels. They enjoy upward mobility. And their style of living improves along with their rise in career and income status. They can buy more creature comforts, save money, invest it, and, at least, believe that they're building security for the future. In addition, middle-class couples have the wherewithal to escape from the tensions and doldrums of daily living, from the confines of their nuclear nests. They can hire baby-sitters and go out for an evening or for a weekend, and take vacations for a complete change of pace.

Members of the working class, blue-collar workers (over forty million of them in America) and low-paid white-collar people do not have upward mobility. With too few exceptions, their jobs lead to nowhere; they face doing the same routine tasks day after day, whether it be in a factory, office, or retail outlet. Though white-collar and service workers have more job security and may be accorded slightly higher social status than blue-collar workers, both remain, to varying degrees, in a financial bind from day one to the end.

Oddly enough, young working-class couples, just prior to marriage, tend to think that they've "got it made," or at least that they will have. He's "making good money," and she may be working, too. Understandably, they marry with hope in the future. But they also marry minus any capital to buy a car, furniture, and, most of all, a home. Result: they start their married life on the installment plan. If they do buy a car, it's financed. So are their appliances, furniture, and color TV. Thus they've immediately obligated themselves to such an extent that leisure activities, such as entertainment and travel, are unaffordable luxuries at the very outset. The time payments have to be made instead.

This is how a thirty-two-year-old man, a grammar school graduate, describes how lack of financial security affected his marriage from the very beginning:

> You keep thinking you can do almost anything and get away with anything when you're still young. There had been a couple of big layoffs when we got married, but work was still pretty good and I thought I could do anything and that I was going places and I was going to be somebody. Nothing was good enough for my wife, and we didn't think nothing of charge

accounts and buying things. We hadn't been married long when I got my first layoff. They said I was young. They laid off others and said they was old. We couldn't keep up our payments on the furniture and we lost every stick of it, and she was pregnant. We went and stayed at her ma's for a few days, and then up to my ma's . . . and my ma had a spare room, and we must have stayed there about a month while I was looking for work and then I got it, and then we moved out again. And then this time, we got one thing by paying the whole money on it that we borrowed the money for. We borrowed from people and not the bank. And we bought a bed. We figured we could sit on that and we had our cooking pots and could eat out of them. But we didn't want to think of sleeping on the floor anymore. It would have been all right if it was summer and she wasn't pregnant.[1]

A thirty-year-old refinery operative, father of three and married for ten years, when asked "Was there some period of adjustment after you were married?" replied:

Was there? Wow! Before I got married, I only had to do for myself; after, there was somebody else all the time. I mean, before, there was my family but that was different. . . . Then, I suddenly found I had to worry about where we'd live and whether we had enough money, all those things like that. Before, I could always get a job and make enough money to take care of me and give something to the house [his parents']. Then, after we got married, I suddenly had all those responsibilities. Before, it didn't make a difference if I didn't feel like going to work sometimes. Then, all of a sudden, it made one hell of a difference because the rent might not get paid or, if it got paid, there might not be enough food money. [2]

Those are examples of how it starts. Then comes the first baby and subsequently more children. This results in increased costs, larger debts, and, at best, a deflated cushion of savings. With one bad break (practically guaranteed)—a cutback in overtime, a temporary layoff, injury or illness—the savings are gone. Temporary though this may be, financial chaos and humiliation take their toll on the relationship. And the constant fear of such dire possibilities is emotionally damaging to husband and wife. As one social scientist describes it: "Although economic well-being does not guarantee marital happiness, economic insecurity is likely to have a profound impact on family relations." [3]

However, many people prefer to believe that there is no connection whatsoever between money and love. To their way of thinking they are as polar opposite as fire and water; they believe that money, akin to water, tends to quench the fires of love. Therefore the richer a family is, the colder its members are to each other. Conversely, those families who have to work, worry, and struggle to make ends meet are bonded together in a supportive, loving relationship.

Unfortunately reality belies this belief. Statistics show that the higher the income, education, and occupation, the less likelihood there is for divorce. There is a far greater incidence of family fission, manifesting itself in desertion or divorce, among the working class. The misconception that divorce was more infrequent among the less economically privileged probably stems from the fact that, some years ago, divorces were expensive to obtain and thus were solely the alternatives of the wealthy. This situation has long ceased to exist.

The main stresses confronting the working class, which annihilate the romantic notion that there's no relationship between love and money, can be categorized as follows:

Economic angst. Angst (stemming from the German word for "fear") is the only word which succinctly describes this emotional state. Worse than fretting and anxiety, it includes a gnawing, stabbing, continual sense of dread. Every blue-collar family may not be confronted with it all the time. But all have, or will have, faced it at some time. Overtly, or covertly, it is a daily part of being. This dread is an opened Pandora's Box of miseries: not being able to meet time payments, not having enough money left to buy enough groceries and clothing for the children, facing the dire possibility of being unable to pay for heat, light, and phone, let alone the rent. Total escape from economic angst is a rarity, if not an impossibility. Its toll is severe on husband and wife and its fallout affects their children as well.

A thirty-four-year-old mother of five, married seventeen years, describes her first few years of marriage:

> The truth is we were just plain poor, dirt poor, and the only thing that got us through was that we used to eat at my parents' almost every day. They couldn't do much for us; they never had much either. But they always had enough food to share even if maybe they all had to eat a little less.
>
> Also, even though I couldn't go out to work, I used to take in ironing and watch some kids. Between it all, we would just manage to get through most of the time. . . . We were luckier than a lot of people we knew, because we didn't have to go down to the welfare like they did.[4]

Job anguish. It would be almost impossible to find one blue-collar worker who had never experienced a period of unemployment, or certainly the threat of joblessness. A thirty-year-old welder, father of four and married eleven years, says:

> Right after our first kid was born, I got laid off, and it looked like it would be a long time before I'd be working again. The company I worked for was cutting back, and I didn't have seniority or anything like that. And I didn't have much in the way of skills to get another job with.

63

My unemployment ran out pretty quick, and Sue Ann couldn't work because of the baby, and she wasn't feeling too good anyhow after the baby came. So we moved in with my folks. We lived there for about a year. What a mess. My mom and Sue Ann just didn't get along.[5]

There are additional corrosive factors which go along with blue-collar work. There's the dead-end monotony of performing the identical task hour after hour, day after day, whether it's on the assembly line or in other kinds of repetitive manual labor. No challenge, no change of pace, practically no chance for advancement. And there's always the foreman or supervisor whose job it is to make sure that the workers perform at maximum capacity to fulfill the production quota. There's also the gnawing certainty that there's no other future but to stay with the job as long as the economy and one's health permit. Chances for advancement exist, to be sure, but they are the exception. The end result of such frustrations and indignities are predictable: They erode a worker's sense of self-esteem.

Included, too, in this bag of "dirty-work tricks" is an additional ego destroyer: joblessness. Blue-collar workers are highly vulnerable to layoffs. The immediate, tangible effect of unemployment is, obviously, financial. But there is a side effect which is almost as devastating: the psychological havoc which permeates the entire family. Blue-collar workers usually blame themselves for their loss of a job and for being unable to find other work; they do not blame the system. In turn, their families have the same reaction. It's not the company, it's not the state of the economy, it's *his* fault. Somehow he's a failure. This combination of shame and blame further erode a worker's self-esteem. And having to be around the home all day, with nothing to do, exacerbates his sense of uselessness. His presence is a source of annoyance to his family.

Thus, contrary to the blissful belief that travail within a

worker's family brings its members closer together, tension ensues instead. This is statistically demonstrated by the following: When Flint, Michigan, suffered a 20 percent unemployment rate during a shutdown of its main industry—automotive plants—alcoholism and child abuse soared. And, although there are no records to substantiate this, wife beating probably increased as well.

Here is how a twenty-six-year-old woman, mother of two, felt about her husband's periodic unemployment:

> I could hardly ever forgive him for getting fired from his job. We never stopped arguing about that. I felt so frightened, I almost couldn't stand it.
>
> . . . I couldn't understand how anybody could get fired from a job . . . my father never got fired from his job. . . . He's always been a real stable man, and he'd never do anything to jeopardize his job.
>
> My husband is not stable that way. He calls in sick a lot. . . . Even now, after we've had things so hard and they're finally beginning to settle down a little, he still does things like that, and I'm always worrying about what will become of us. . . .[6]

I want to quote from another case study from Mirra Komarovsky's book *Blue-Collar Marriage*. Although it depicts the ultimate in working-class family miseries, it also illustrates many of the lesser misfortunes experienced by most working-class families.

The wife, who is thirty-seven years old and mother of seven children, has to do piece work at home so that the family, including an ailing mother-in-law, can survive. The husband is a maintenance worker whose take-home pay is meager. The wife's day starts at six in the morning, and her work does not cease until eight-thirty in the evening when she hopes that "it might let up a little so that I could put my feet up. I try to see that my husband and kids have enough to eat. Sometimes he yells at me when I ain't got enough and I tell him I do the best I can." [7]

During a number of in-depth interviews she, and then her husband, were specifically asked about their sexual relations and attitudes toward family planning. Both of them being Protestant, the large size of their family was puzzling. Here is a direct quote from the book:

> The wife herself was one of seven children and she attributed the poverty of her parental home to the large size of the family. After her fourth child was born she told the doctor she simply couldn't stand having any more. The doctor "was afraid to tell her because of the Catholics in their community," so she had gone to the neighboring town and got fitted out with a pessary [a device to prevent conception].
>
> "We paid eight dollars for all that junk and a fat lot of good it did us. . . . The thing is, I'd have to wear it all the time, and I can't. It hurts me. I went back to the doctor about it, and he said it wasn't safe to wear all the time, I might give myself a cancer. . . . You never know when the fit is going to come on him [her husband]. He seems to know when I got it on and not bother me and then the minute I take it off, he seems to know and comes for me."

This is the balance of this interview verbatim:

Q: Why do you let him then? / A: What else can I do?

Q: Can't you tell him to wait a minute? / A: Yea, but he don't want to.

Q: Does he want children? / A: He don't care.

Q: What do you think makes him this way? / A: I don't know.

Q: Is he rough with you? / A: No, not exactly. Not like the others I hear about.

66

Q: Well, why don't you make him wait? / A: I wouldn't feel right about it.

Q: Are there a lot of women in the same fix with you around here? / A: Yea, I guess so, most of them, I guess.

Q: Haven't you heard of women who managed to get their husbands to be more considerate? / A: Yea, I guess they're better fixed with money.

Q: What's it got to do with money? / A: Well, I guess when a man's got other pleasures, he ain't so selfish about this one.

Q: Do other women feel that way around here? / A: Yea, a lot of them do. They say they pity the men. That's the only thing they got. Most of the people's Catholics, and they say it goes against God if you don't give in to a man and give him his one pleasure.

Q: Well, he does have other pleasures. He smokes cigars and he looks to me like he eats a lot too. / A: Yea, he smokes all the time, and he gets more than he needs to eat.

Q: Does he get more to eat than the children do? / A: I try to see that they get enough to eat, but he says that he's got to eat to keep his strength up so he can work so they can all have something to eat. So he gets the best of it. Sometimes I keeps some back and feed them after he's gone.

Q: But you're not Catholic, and don't you think that it's wrong to have children if you can't bring them up right? / A: Yea, sometimes it bothers me real bad. I get scared if I don't feed them right, like they'll get sick and maybe die. I think maybe that's a sin too.

Q: Do you know other people whose husbands are nice to them, nicer than yours? / A: Yea, but they ain't so busy, they ain't got so many kids to feed.

Q: Well, then why does he keep making more kids? /
A: I don't know. I asked him about it a couple of times and he didn't say nothing.[8]

One would think that this woman would feel bitter toward her husband, but such was not the case. Her bitterness was directed against "fate" more than against him. She summed up her attitude in these words: "We gotta decent family. I always say thank God. He's real steady and good on his job. He don't run around with other women. He ain't so bad about my takin' on work. He knows I gotta do it. I know one man who beats up his wife because she goes to work, but they can't eat without it." [9]

The husband's attitude toward their situation was expressed as follows when he was asked what he thought made for a good marriage:

A man's gotta live his life and do his job. He's gotta think about the whole family and not just himself. Not all the fellows bring home their pay straight to their wives, but I think that makes things a lot simpler. It don't do no good to cut up and drink a lot of beer on payday. You just put off the grief that way. It's better to go out and have a beer when you enjoy it and after you've done the things that have to be done most. A man shouldn't say one thing one time and another, another. It gets the kids upset. He's gotta be strong and stick to his word. He shouldn't be afraid to put his foot down when it's going to do some good.

The wife ought to do her duty and I don't rightly know how to say what her duty is, except that you can tell when she's doin' it. And you want her to do it right, and not be a sourpuss about it. I tell the girls to do their work and keep at it until it's done and not to go poopin' around all over the place but to stick to it and get it over with. After that they can play and they can enjoy it more. I guess that holds true right into married life. Sometimes you get more on your hands

68

than you know how to handle. A good wife has to be able to take it when times like that comes along.[10]

Monetary worries, coupled with unemployment, bring about frustration, friction, and acute misery in marriage. And there's one segment of our population, 12 percent, who are habitually exposed to them: blacks. With proportionately few exceptions, they are confined to the working-class's lowest-paying job brackets. Despite the efforts of some dedicated people to eradicate racial discrimination and prejudice, their quality of life remains shockingly substandard. They have to cope with the harsh realities of our economic and social system with a genetic handicap: blackness. If you have a black face, you face discrimination in every field of endeavor. Blacks in the professions and managerial fields receive lower pay than whites. Craftsmen, foremen, and similar workers receive less pay than their white counterparts. And getting a job is many times more difficult for a black man or woman. Proportionately, over twice as many blacks as whites are currently unemployed.

Consequently, relatively more black than white families are on welfare. However, our welfare aid to underprivileged families has often had the effect of splitting families apart. The AFDC (Aid to Families with Dependent Children) was carefully designed to help children whose fathers were not living at home. A black family with an unemployed father who lived with them was not eligible for financial assistance. As a result, many low-income black fathers have been forced to desert their families so that their wives and children could receive welfare aid.

The effects of these negative stresses have had predictable results on blacks' marriage and family life. For example, the odds are that one out of every two black women will be divorced. This compares with one out of three for their white counterparts. To confirm the fact that money makes the marry-go-round go, the divorce rate for higher-income black families, the middle class, is discernibly lower. The high rate of unemployment, combined with urban chaos, violence, and poverty, have resulted in many black men never marrying and many black fathers deserting their families. As of recent years, 36 percent of all black children live with only one parent. The combined social stresses faced by our black citizens undermine their marital and family relations with a vengeance.

Up to this point you have been exposed to the negatives involved in marriage. They are realities which must be faced but may not, however, cancel the positives. However, your reaction may be: "It seems to me that, whether I'm a member of the middle or working class, my chances for marital happiness seem limited."

True.

"Then why should I consider marriage at all?"

For a number of valid reasons. (1) Regardless of what you now know about matrimonial hazards, the chances are nine out of ten that you are going to get married anyway. (2) The single life, especially for the male, seems to be less rewarding than married life under our present social conditions. (3) Living together instead of marrying not only involves identical relationship problems between a man and a woman, but is also stripped of the societal and legal commitments involved in marriage.

In short, the institution of marriage, was, is, and, for the foreseeable future, ever shall be. Therefore the ensuing chapters are devoted to preparing you to make the best of the inevitable. Furthermore, there *are* happily married couples, even though they are more the exception than the rule. How and with whom can you try to achieve a happy union? That is what we shall now explore.

SOURCE NOTES FOR CHAPTER VI:

1. Mirra Komarovsky, *Blue-Collar Marriage* (New York: Vintage Books, 1967), p. 47.

2. Lillian Breslow Rubin, *Worlds of Pain* (New York: Basic Books, 1976), p. 70.
3. Skonlik, *The Intimate Environment,* p. 149.
4. Rubin, *Worlds of Pain,* p. 74.
5. Ibid., p. 73.
6. Ibid., pp. 76–77.
7. Komarovsky, *Blue-Collar Marriage,* p. 65.
8. Ibid., pp. 89–92.
9. Ibid., p. 92.
10. Ibid., p. 92.

VII
THE THREE
PREMARITAL HEXES

Before we delve into the specific problems involved in choosing a marital mate, there are three fundamental problem areas which have to be discussed in detail. They are: gender-role stereotyping, the meaning of love, and the role of sex. Money, religious differences, life-style, personal goals and ambitions, and sense of self fall more easily into place once these three basics are understood.

The quagmire of gender-role stereotyping

In recent years more and more books and articles have been published aimed at enlightening women as to their proper, versus their traditionally limited roles. Feminist writers have tried to make their sisters aware of the fact that they should regard themselves as persons rather than as females. Even the "master sex," the male, is being cautioned to regard phony concepts of maleness and self-limiting in addition to being destructive to women.

However, despite these attempts to dry up the quagmire of gender-role stereotyping, the traditions of the past continue to exert their negative influences and are apparent in parental and peer-group attitudes. It should not be surprising, therefore, if you find that you are still under the spell of this hex. And faulty beliefs about what it means to be a woman or man are guaranteed to impede a meaningful, durable heterosexual and subsequent marital relationship. Since both sexes need to break through sex-role barriers, the subject need not be divided into "his" and "ms" departments like public washrooms.

Young men and women share a fundamental problem: coping with the business of Being in the most rewarding manner possible; rewarding to self and to others. To accomplish this goal requires a sound appreciation of your human rights. Ideally, learning about these ought to start in early childhood. But let's be realistic, it seldom does. Little children learn about themselves, about others, about behaving like a boy or girl, from their parents.[1]

Since we are solely concerned with the subject of marriage, I am merely going to pose a few questions and answers in order to stimulate you to think further on the subject. If you find that you have some serious hangups about gender-role behavior, the bibliography lists some books on the subject which may be consulted.

Is it as important for a young woman, as for a young man, to get a college degree in order to qualify for a professional or business career? Or is it more of a luxury than a necessity since, with minor exceptions, a woman is going to be a wife and mother?

It is just as much a woman's privilege as a man's to get a degree. Regardless of whether she will marry and have children, she should have the right of developing herself to optimum capacity in order to enjoy a sense of self-fulfillment and, from the practical standpoint, so that she may be economically independent. Furthermore, married or not, most women will be employed for many years. The United States Department of Labor's data indicates that over half of today's high school girls will work full-time for as many as thirty years of their lives, and 90 percent will be employed other long periods of time. At present, women compose almost 50 percent of the labor force. Furthermore, 10 percent of family heads (those on whom families depend for support) are women. And, whether a woman is a member of the economically privileged class or of the lower-income class, marriage and parenthood are not mandatory goals. She should consider her *personhood* as her paramount objective, whether single or wedded.

But since nature has programmed women, biologically and physiologically, for bearing, giving birth to, and nurturing children, shouldn't she regard this as her primary obligation, especially since a man cannot perform these basic functions?

Today, the comparatively easy availability of contraceptives as well as abortion, give a woman control over her body: She can choose whether or not to have children. Furthermore, there is no evidence to substantiate the traditional belief that a woman will feel incomplete unless she has a child. Some may and do, but this is the result of social tradition rather than a natural mission. With the growing opportunities for women to enter both the professions and the business world, their potentials for self-fulfillment are no longer dependent on parturition. If a woman opts to have a child, she can resume her career activities soon after giving birth, and rely on day-care centers to tend her baby.

Males are, by nature, more aggressive, more competitive, and physically stronger than women. Therefore isn't it the male's correctly assigned role to be the family breadwinner and dominant member in the marriage relationship?

These are faulty concepts. Neither geneticists nor behavioral scientists have resolved the question of whether the human male is more aggressive and the female more sociable and nurturant. To date they have found no clearcut way to

77

draw the line between environmental influences and prede-
termination. As social scientist, Helen Block Lewis, states it:

> Many observed differences between men and women
> can in fact readily be related to social expectations of
> them and to women's inferior status. Since the heredi-
> tary psychological differences that come with the sexual
> differentiation are, in fact, as yet almost completely un-
> known, speculation about them has seemed pointless
> and easily put to the use of justifying women's inferior
> social position.[2]

Eros, agape, love, and confusion

Love is probably the most misunderstood, abused, over-
used word in our language. Whether it's referred to as *eros*
("sensual love") *agape* ("selfless, spiritual love"), or just
love, its meaning is grounded in so much confusion that it may
never be resolved to everyone's entire satisfaction. In today's
society, love is supposed to be *the* basis for a "happy marriage." This is a comparatively recent assumption. In Grecian
times, especially in the fourth and fifth centuries B.C., love
played no part in courtship or marriage. Instead, love occurred
between married men and *hetaera* (educated prostitutes), or
between men and young boys. Because of women's vastly inferior social position, a heterosexual relationship excluded
love as a prime motivational factor.

On the other hand, the Romans acknowledged that love
was an important element in a heterosexual relationship—not
within marriage, however, but in extramarital, adulterous relationships in which it served as a form of bait or lure. This
attitude is dramatically demonstrated in Ovid's work *The Art
of Love,* written in the first century A.D. He describes love as
a carefully planned series of maneuvers to conquer a member
of the opposite sex. As an amusing example, this is how he
suggests a man can succeed while being a spectator at a horse
race:

Furthermore, don't overlook the meetings when horses are running: / In the crowds at the track opportunity waits. / There is no need for a code of finger-signals or nodding. / Sit as close as you like; no one will stop you at all. / In fact, you will have to sit close—that's one of the rules, at a racetrack. / Whether she likes it or not, contact is part of the game. / Try to find something in common, to open the conversation; / Don't care too much what you say, just so that everyone hears; / Ask her, "Whose colors are those?"—that's good for an opening gambit.

. . . Often it happens that dust may fall on the blouse of the lady. / If such dust should fall, carefully brush it away. / Even if there's no dust, brush off whatever there isn't. / Any excuse will do: why do you think you have hands? / If her cloak hangs low, and the ground is getting it dirty, / Gather it up with care, lift it a little, so! / Maybe, by way of reward, and not without her indulgence, / You'll be able to see ankle or possibly knee.

. . . Such is the chance of approach the racetrack can offer a lover.[3]

The Middle Ages introduced a new kind of love: *courtly love*. It was a mixed bag of strange contradictions: adulterous passion, Christian religious devotion, flirting games and serious moral purposes, betrayal, faithlessness, joy, and suffering.

Marriages were arranged based on property rights and social status and had little or nothing to do with mutual love. Consequently love was channeled to extramarital adventures. During the age of chivalry, "well-born" women (dubbed "ladies") were placed on a pseudopedestal. This attitude did not elevate a woman, but limited her needs and capacities instead. However, it did initiate a hitherto unheard of concept, rarely accorded women in Eastern cultures: a limited respect for them rather than looking upon them as mere pieces of property.

Courtly love, also called romantic love, has remained a dominant theme in heterosexual relationships to this very day. It manifested itself in the bourgeois marriages of the eighteenth century. And when industrialism superseded an agricultural society in the Western World, the concept of romantic love spread to the working class as well.

The "romantic love complex," as some call it, remains very much a part of our American culture, for better or for worse. Most authors of marriage texts emphasize "real," "true," or "mature" love in contrast to romantic love. The latter is associated with such emotional hangups as infatuation and "love at first sight." Although some marriage experts (if there are such) have had a few kind words to say about romantic love as part of our social structure, none seem to think that it is the basis for a satisfactory marriage relationship. It is even suggested that the greater a person's emotional maladjustment, the more likely he or she is to be deluded by the romantic love complex.

Brushing aside "romantic love" as an expendable item leaves us with "true love" and "mature love." But what do they mean? And why has the very concept of love remained so ingrained in our society, where independence, individualism, and self-liberation have assumed primary importance? Our sophisticated technological advances have made it increasingly possible for a person to be economically independent, to be self-reliant rather than other-reliant. But it has also created a far more impersonal world. We are surrounded by strangers, particularly in city living, and confronted with stresses which are difficult to cope with on one's own. Result: it has made people crave intimate relationships. They yearn for someone who will provide sympathy and who will share the burdens of being.

Fear of loneliness itself is another strong motivating force which impels people, often frantically, to seek out others. Our almost exclusively industrial life-style heightens this fear in numerous ways. The end of the extended family, indigenous to an agricultural society, and the substitution of the nuclear family has set people apart. Parents and their children have become a unit removed from grandparents, aunts, uncles, and other relatives. That's divisive step number one. Furthermore, when children in the nuclear family reach adolescence, they are encouraged to relinquish their attachment to their parents and to seek emotional nourishment from others: from girlfriends, boyfriends, "best friends"—from their peer group. As they grow older such emotional attachments combine with sexual yearnings so that (in most instances) a person of the opposite sex assumes the dual role of satisfying the emotional and sexual needs. At this point love enters the picture whether it's true love, real love, mature love, or merely the transference of self-need to another in one's frantic desire to escape being on one's own and alone.

Now comes the crucial question: How are you supposed to decide whether you are "truly" in love? Research shows that people usually fall in love several times before they marry. Were they "truly" in love each time? And romantic love notions to the contrary, love doesn't happen suddenly: "Our eyes met, locked, and that was it." Evidence shows that falling in love is a gradual process—getting acquainted with someone followed by numerous repeat encounters. Writes social scientist Arlene Skolnik:

> Many people report growing to love someone whom they did not find overwhelmingly attractive in the first place, but with whom they developed deep rapport and enjoyable companionship . . . more than half the married men and women [in a survey] said they had no strong physical attraction until at least two months after they had met.[4]

Up to this point the word "love" still has not been defined. Trying to define "good" is difficult enough as it involves personal judgment, cultural values, and unconscious emotional pulls. Trying to explain the meaning of love is more difficult because emotion plays a far more dominant role. Psychologists, psychiatrists, and other social theorists have tried to delineate its affirmative aspects and have warned against its delusionary ones. The following are two good examples:

> The delight of two people in one another, "in an atmosphere of security based on mutuality, reciprocity, and trust. . . ." If this sort of intimacy develops and persists over the years, Dr. Calderone suggests, neither the major physical infirmities, nor aging, nor fading of physical handsomeness, nor reduced sexual potency, nor even infidelity will destroy the relationship. "In intimacy two people are constantly saying to each other without words, I delight in you as a whole person and you delight me. . . .[5]

Here is the second description by the famous psychiatrist Erich Fromm:

> Infantile love follows the principle: *"I love because I am loved."* Mature love follows the principle: *"I am loved because I love."* Immature love says: *"I love you because I need you."* Mature love says: *"I need you because I love you."* [6]

The foregoing quotations are not offered as definitive explanations nor did their authors intend them to be. But they can serve as hints and guidelines.

There is little doubt that *"wanting to feel loved"* is a stronger pull than *"wanting to love."* The former, the passive attitude, is subject to more pitfalls than the active drive of wanting to love another. It can create a parasitic relationship: a taking, not giving; loss of self-identity and complete dependency. Such parasitism is in direct contrast to a symbiotic relationship in which two dissimilar organisms—you and your mate—live together in a mutually supportive relationship.

On the other hand, yearning to love another person may

be a compulsive drive in some individuals. They feel incomplete, miserable, lost if they do not find a love object. Such a compulsion has serious repercussions and probably originates from the person's total lack of self-esteem. This is what propels him or her to seek completeness in someone else. A sense of completeness and self-esteem must come from self, never from another person. A meaningful other can reaffirm, reassure, but never restructure your essential self.

What is love's role in the heterosexual and marital relationship? Being that love is such an ephemeral, often illusory, almost indefinable emotional state, some young people put their trust in more tangible factors: companionship, mutual interests, compatibility, respect, and mutually satisfactory sex. This does not mean that love plays no part in the relationship, but it evolves from, rather than causes, an affirmative, enduring relationship. A study of two thousand engaged couples seems to confirm this. Two-thirds of the men and three-quarters of the women were able to mention defects about their mates. In other words, love did not blind them because it developed *from* their realistically based, intimate relationships.

Social theorists have also found that love does not conquer all. It seldom crosses class barriers. The large majority of marriages take place between men and women in the same socioeconomic class, religion, educational level, and even the same level of physical attractiveness. A homely person generally pairs with a homely person. It is comparatively rare that an exceptionally physically attractive person will bond with a far less attractive mate.

The hex of sex

In general, the word "sex" no longer has a scatalogical connotation. Nor is "having sex" looked upon as a "dirty" act. That's because of the sexual revolution which, however, might more aptly be called our sexual evolution. The more enlightened attitudes toward premarital sex, extramarital sex, homosexual sex, and self-sex have come about gradually. Thus it has been more of an evolutionary rather than revolutionary process. Also, sexual enlightenment has not penetrated completely: Most parents still avoid discussing sex with their children, and sex education in many schools is still at "the birds and bees" stage with a pinch of anatomy, physiology, and the dangers of venereal disease thrown in.

On the other hand, the mass media, movies, and the thrust of much consumer advertising use sex as their prime lure. Social theorists' books on the subject have covered it from almost every conceivable angle. There are books on the joys of autoeroticism, volume upon volume on the hundreds of different ways to attain ultimate pleasure in heterosexual sex (copiously illustrated with photos), and even books on the joys of homosexual lovemaking.

Our sexual revolution has made significant progress in liberating sex from religious taboos and societal stigma. The feminist movement, the Kinsey studies and those of sexologists Masters and Johnson, have put woman's sexuality in a more realistic context. With all of this enlightenment one would think that "all's well in the bedroom." But that is not exactly the case.

> . . . Like Victorian doctrines about the dangers and ugliness of sex, modern ideas about sex as healthy and good are, above all, just that—a set of ideas. . . . There is no denying that, for many people, the sexual revolution has brought about greater freedom, pleasure, and mutuality in sex. Yet at the same time, the new legitimation of sex and the new standard of sexual performance can create new tensions and anxieties.[7]

Lillian Rubin, whose study of working-class women you read about in the previous chapter, found that many of them reacted negatively to the new sexual freedom. Their husbands' demands for oral sex were oppressive, and they often felt disassociated from their own orgasms. She also interviewed upper-middle-class women and found that they and their husbands were far more relaxed about sexual attitudes. But they frequently had a sense of guilt about not being able to overcome their inhibitions and live up to the new standards of sexual freedom. They blamed themselves for what they felt was their inadequacy in sexual adjustment.

Apparently, the new sexual freedom has not necessarily opened up new vistas of limitless pleasure. Instead, it has raised the standards of satisfaction to such a degree that many feel inadequate because they cannot meet the prescribed rules for "good sex." For example, the major complaints of people who go to sex clinics is that they cannot get "turned on" as much as they would like. A not uncommon complaint of men and women in college is that they are made uncomfortable by the new standards of sexual frequency and intensity. Psychiatrists are finding that on campus and in general the male's sexual drive is often being thwarted by impotence. He is unable to perform in the new sexual climate, and this is exacerbated by the increasing assertiveness of women.

> Assuming the existence of adequate venereal hygiene and efficient, readily available contraception, what, if any, is the danger of this new situation? The answer, as some have seen it, is the "tyranny of the orgasm," the need created by the social pressures of the new permissive convention to achieve maximum copulatory performance. This is seen as a threat to the person who truly falls in love, but who is incapable of sufficiently impressive orgasmic achievements.[8]

The negatives resulting from the new sexual freedom do not in any way justify reversing our sexual evolution's progress. One should be aware that it is still in a formative phase and that the forces of religious and cultural atavism are creating many of the hangups. As our sexual evolution continues to progress, its extremes will be mitigated. Furthermore, the new sexual freedom does not seem to have destroyed love. Instead, with sex so readily available, it has allowed for a greater intimacy which, in turn, can lead to a relationship which is not solely dependent on sexual performance. Our sexual evolution has started to change the rules and meanings of love, sex, and marriage, it is hoped for the better.

SOURCE NOTES FOR CHAPTER VII:

1. Robert H. Loeb, Jr., *Breaking the Sex-Role Barrier* (New York: Franklin Watts, Inc., 1977), p. 5.
2. Helen Block Lewis, *Psychic War in Men and Women* (New York University Press, 1976), pp. 38–40.
3. Rolfe Humphries (translator), *Ovid: The Art of Love* (Indiana University Press, 1957), pp. 109–110.
4. Skolnik, *The Intimate Environment,* p. 210.
5. James Leslie McCary, *Human Sexuality* (New York: Van Nostrand Co., Inc., 1973), pp. 294–295.
6. Erich Fromm, *The Art of Loving* (New York: Harper & Row, 1956), p. 34.
7. Skolnik, *The Intimate Environment,* p. 194.
8. Desmond Morris, *Intimate Behavior* (New York: Random House, 1971), p. 86.

VIII
HOW TO AND NOT TO "I DO"

We are now at the point where we can put the knowledge of how marriage operated in the past, the stresses involved in blue-collar and middle-class marriage, directly to work for you. Having pierced the fog of myth and wishful thinking, you should be in a position to evaluate marriage more objectively and realistically.

However, to explore the prospect of matrimony as it relates to you and your future requires subjecting yourself to some candid self-examination. Its purpose is to help you evaluate your level of emotional and intellectual maturity. In order to accomplish this you are going to take on a dual role: as "patient" and as "premarital counselor."

In order to make this as specific and relevant as possible, the questions you will confront have been sex-segregated into His and Ms. They are limited to a few basics and do not pretend to approach all the questions you should ask yourself. It is hoped they will set off a chain reaction so that you ask yourself many more. To derive maximum benefit from this quiz it is vital that your yes or no answers be given with complete candor. Don't allow yourself to be influenced by what you think is "supposed to be" the right response.

The correct replies, with explanations, are listed at the end of each quiz. It's easy enough to determine whether you have passed or failed your premarital exam. If you find that you have more wrong than right answers, you need to do some rethinking and reevaluation about yourself and your beliefs. This can prove to be a growth experience. In fairness I must state that there is no absolute "right" answer, no categorical truth. But you can approach a functional truth (one that seems to be viable) by subjecting your beliefs to severe scrutiny. The famous seventeenth-century philosopher Descartes said: *"Dubito ergo sum"* ("I doubt, therefore I am").

His Quiz

1. Do you feel that the only way you can give your life a real purpose is to get married?

   (　)yes 　　　　(　)no

2. Would you marry a woman who considered her career as important as yours?

   (　)yes 　　　　(　)no

3. Do you feel that the only way to assure yourself that the woman you love is yours is by marrying her?

   (　)yes 　　　　(　)no

4. Do you think that getting married will help you find yourself?

   (　)yes 　　　　(　)no

5. Do you believe that the primary thing a wife can offer you is satisfactory, available sex?

   (　)yes 　　　　(　)no

6. When married, would you rely mainly on your male friends for companionship?

   (　)yes 　　　　(　)no

7. Would the prospect of living by yourself for a period of time greatly disturb you?

   (　)yes 　　　　(　)no

8. Would you refuse to marry a woman, even though you

loved her, if you discovered that she had had sexual relations with other men before she met you?

( )yes ( )no

9. Do you feel uncomfortable with a woman whom you consider your intellectual equal or superior?

( )yes ( )no

10. Do you think that contraception is a woman's responsibility?

( )yes ( )no

11. If you and your wife had jobs, would you nevertheless think it was "unmanly" for you to share the cooking, housework, and child caring?

( )yes ( )no

12. Would you marry someone you loved even if your family disapproved of the marriage?

( )yes ( )no

13. Do you find it easier to talk openly about your problems with your men friends than with the woman you intend marrying?

( )yes ( )no

14. Do you fear that falling in love with someone will cause you to lose your identity?

( )yes ( )no

15. Do you think that having a child will make a faltering marriage relationship more solid?

( )yes ( )no

16. If your wife had an extramarital affair, would you be able to accept it?

( )yes ( )no

Ms. Quiz

1. Do you feel that the only way you can give your life a real purpose is to get married?

( )yes ( )no

2. Would you refuse to marry a man who insisted that his career take precedence over yours?

( ) yes   ( ) no

3. Do you think that getting married is the best and surest way for you to achieve economic security?

( ) yes   ( ) no

4. Do you think that getting married will help you find yourself?

( ) yes   ( ) no

5. Do you think that the most important thing a husband can offer you is a sense of protection?

( ) yes   ( ) no

6. When married, would you rely primarily on your female friends for companionship?

( ) yes   ( ) no

7. Would the prospect of living by yourself for a period of time greatly disturb you?

( ) yes   ( ) no

8. Would you refuse to marry a man if he told you that he might have extramarital affairs?

( ) yes   ( ) no

9. Do you prefer a man whom you consider your intellectual superior?

( ) yes   ( ) no

10. Do you think that contraception should be a shared responsibility?

( ) yes   ( ) no

11. Do you think that a man has the right to refuse to let his woman friend or wife have an abortion if she so wishes?

( ) yes   ( ) no

12. Would you marry a man you loved even if your family disapproved of the marriage?

( ) yes   ( ) no

13. Would you think less of a man if he needed to share his problems with you?

( ) yes   ( ) no

14. Do you fear that falling in love with someone will cause you to lose your identity?

     ( )yes   ( )no

15. Do you think that having a child will make a faltering marriage relationship more solid?

     ( )yes   ( )no

16. Would you feel resentful if your husband refused a better-paying job because he felt it would not be fulfilling for him?

     ( )yes   ( )no

His Quiz Answers and Comments

1. NO—Trying to find a purpose in life, a rewarding reason for being, is not easy. And if you limit it to *having* rather than to *doing,* to possessions obtainable by what you earn, you are limiting your potential for self-fulfillment. A purpose in life is more likely to be achieved by what, to you, seems soul-satisfying and meaningful. It is for you to find or create this goal. To rely on marriage to give you a purpose in life is not only self-limiting, but places an impossible burden upon your wife and is bound to fail. Marriage was not designed to be a form of psychological intensive care.

2. YES—There is no logical, biological, or ethical reason why a woman's career should not be as important as a man's. This includes her right, if affordable, to a college education and, if she wishes, to post-graduate schooling so that she will be able to compete in the job market. You have no preordained prerogative to place your goals ahead of your wife's and to expect her to follow in your wake.

3. NO—If you think that by marrying you will make the woman you love your exclusive possession, an object branded "private property—keep off," you have a problem. It's probably rooted in a lack of self-esteem: You cannot believe that she loves and respects you because

93

you don't respect yourself. Obviously, marriage will not resolve that problem, most certainly not if your distrust of her has validity.

4. NO—But a qualified no. Ideally when contemplating marriage, you ought to be well enough grounded in your self not to need someone else to help you find your bearings. You've already been made aware of the dangers resulting from *needing* someone in order to feel complete. In marriage, two halves do not make a whole. On the other hand, loving someone and feeling loved in return can, in some instances, be the affirmative interplay which creates a more positive attitude toward one's self.

5. NO—If your prime reason for getting married is that you're tired of constantly chasing around for a "sure thing" sex partner, your expectations from marriage are limited indeed. Marriage, to be rewarding and durable, involves love, companionship, trust, and a sharing in all the ramifications of being.

6. NO—As stated above, one of the prime bonds between wife and husband is shared companionship. This includes mutual cultural and recreational interests. If you're going to rely on your men friends to provide this, to the exclusion of your wife, you are relegating her to being a household convenience and depriving both her and yourself of a rewarding life experience. That's what marriage is supposed to be. Don't rob it of its potential.

7. NO—Being able to live by yourself, without a sense of panic about loneliness, requires emotional maturity and stability. Recent studies of loneliness indicate that it does not come from being alone. Instead, it is the result of the individual's *interpretation* of his or her situation rather than the actual circumstances. And this interpretation appears to be directly related to childhood experiences involving divorce: "The older a child is when his or her parents divorce, the less lonely he is likely to be as an adult . . . people who were younger than six years of age

when their parents separated got the highest scores on the loneliness scale; people who were in middle childhood got lower scores; but people who were adolescent or older were the least lonely as adults." [1]

And consider this: One can feel a dreadful sense of loneliness in a crowd, in a home in which there is limited communication, in an unsatisfactory heterosexual relationship. Thus, getting married in order not to have to live alone is not *the* solution for loneliness, and being able to live alone first offers assurance that you are well grounded in self.

8. NO—But with qualifications. If you refrained from sexual intercourse prior to marriage, a yes response might be understandable. But in today's climate of sexual freedom this is most unlikely. Many men feel that it's their right to have sexual relations prior to marriage but do not extend that privilege to their brides. This is a distinctly sexist attitude and is a carry-over from the past. In those times a bride was considered a piece of property selected with the distinct understanding that "it" hadn't been used by anyone else. It is suggested that you and the woman you intend to marry enter the relationship with no buried secrets about your pasts. If you cannot accept hers, then there's something lacking in the relationship or in your attitude toward women.

9. NO—To prefer a woman whom you can dominate intellectually stems from a number of bad reasons. It can be the result of male chauvinism: A woman is not supposed to be as intelligent as a man and if she is, she's both a threat and a deviant. But it can also stem from a lack of self-assurance on your part, a fragile ego which might be bolstered by psychological counseling.

10. NO—It is not a woman's responsibility to avoid pregnancy. It is a shared one and should be worked out together. Unfortunately, the majority of men absolve themselves from this responsibility for the following reasons.

In the past, woman's second-class status denied her, among other things, the right to control her body. To have sex, to have or not to have a child were a man's decisions. When the completely male dominated medical profession paid serious attention to birth control methods, it devised contraceptive devices for women, not men: the IUD, the birth control pill, the diaphragm, and vaginal jellies. With the exception of the condom (and ancient device) and vasectomy, the male has been spared from an active role in contraception. In other words, the medical profession has concentrated on female precautions. But this, in no way, implies that it should be the woman's responsibility.

11. NO—At this point in the book you probably know that no is the correct answer, assuming you are both working. But face it honestly and if you feel, as many men continue to do, that domestic chores would threaten your concept of maleness, you ought to do some more reading on sex-role stereotyping in order to free yourself from such hangups.

12. YES—But with a few reservations. The usual reasons for family objections stem from religious or ethnic prejudices. For example, if your family is Catholic and she is of the Jewish, or Protestant, or of no faith, they might object. Conversely, if they are of the Jewish faith and she is a Christian, they might object. Or if they are WASPS and she is Italian, black, Polish, Chinese, or Japanese, they might offer objections. In all such instances you should feel secure enough in your love and respect for each other to completely disregard such biases on your family's part. If they raise doubts, it might be advisable to consult a professional trained in marriage counseling.

However, there could be valid causes for family objections. If, for example, neither you nor your prospective bride have adequate earnings to support yourselves without financial aid from your parents, their disapproval

96

would be understandable. You've learned about the role that money plays in a marital relationship and how the lack thereof can erode it. If your family's objections are based upon their belief that either or both of you are not emotionally stable enough to sustain each other, such a doubt ought to be heeded by consulting a marriage counselor.

13. NO—Difficulty and reluctance to communicate with the woman you think you love signals some problems. One could be the fear that, by sharing your anxieties or other causes of unhappiness, you would lose your façade as the strong, fearless male. This is pure traditional fiction. Or, your reluctance might be based upon the false belief that women are less capable of dealing with the realities of a "man's world." Regardless of the underlying cause, you are shutting the door on one of the prime bonds of matrimony: communication and trust.

14. NO—If you fear that by loving someone you will surrender your self and lose your identity, you are not ready for marriage. A loving relationship is not self-surrender. It is a balanced interchange between two individuals without a sense of loss. This does not necessarily guarantee that the relationship will last forever, but it is the essential bond.

15. NO—And a most emphatic no. Too many couples make the mistake of having a child when their relationship is faltering in the belief that parenthood will heal their woes. This is a disastrous concept. An infant is not some superglue which will bond two unhappy people. Having a child under those circumstances will more than likely worsen the rift by creating additional problems. Worse yet, the child will eventually suffer from the emotional turbulence.

16. YES—But a most qualified yes. A sensible reaction would have to depend upon several factors: the kind of marriage you entered into, and the circumstances leading to

the occurrence. If you initially agreed upon an *open marriage*—to be described in the subsequent chapter—then such a happenstance is not supposed to be upsetting, but acceptable. This, in itself, is problematic. If there was no such prior agreement and your wife not only made certain that you learned about the affair, but described its joyful aspects, you would have a valid reason for feeling distressed and for questioning the soundness of your relationship. Marriage counseling would be very much in order. On the other hand, if your wife assured you that it had been an incident with no emotional undertones and no desire for repetition, acceptance would be most feasible provided that you had previously enjoyed a loving relationship. Some counseling might be helpful in order to understand why the incident occurred.

Ms. Quiz Answers and Comments

1. NO—For the same reasons stated in the His Quiz.
2. YES—There is no justifiable reason why a woman should downgrade herself and limit her goals for the sake of a man. And no man who loves you should expect this of you. Ultimately, your sense of self-fulfillment will depend more on what you *do* than upon whom you live with.
3. NO—In the "good old days" when women were openly discriminated against in the business world and in the professions, marriage seemed to be the only way for a woman to assure herself of economic security. Today, thanks to the feminist movement, women have far more opportunities to be independent of male support. If you look upon marriage as the easy way to financial survival, you are not only shortchanging yourself, but taking a poor risk. This is so because the chances are better than one out of three that you'll end up divorced from your breadwinner anyway and you will be left inadequately equipped to cope with self-support.
4. NO—For the same reasons stated in the His Quiz.

5. NO—You should be liberated from gender-role restrictions. The person you ought to rely upon for protection is yourself. Feeling male-dependent is both self-limiting and self-defeating. Furthermore, if you enter marriage believing that you'll be nestling in a cocoon which will insulate you from the hazards, tensions, and evils of the outside world, you're in for a rude awakening. And consider this: it's more likely that a man needs protection—protection from the macho world of overconsumption and overkill which male power has created.
6. NO—For the same reasons stated in the His Quiz.
7. NO—For the same reasons stated in the His Quiz.
8. NO—But with some qualifications. If in a frank and open discussion of your future marriage, he stated that he could not guarantee a lifetime of sexual fidelity because it would be unrealistic, this makes sense, providing, of course, that he would accept the identical reaction from you. If, on the other hand, he made the statement based upon his belief that a man has the right and the need for sexual diversification, but that this does not apply to a woman, you have cause for doubts and refusal to marry him.
9. NO—It is understandable if you find it stimulating to be in the company of people whom you think of as intellectually superior because you find it stimulating. But if you confine this attitude to a man because you think it's your place as a woman to play "dumb" and that you might bruise his ego if you showed equal or superior intelligence, you're using inferiority as a ruse and playing a sexist game.
10. YES—For the same reasons stated in the His Quiz.
11. NO—The reasons for this should be obvious, and especially if you're not married to the man. It is estimated that 10 percent of American women will become pregnant during their high school years. The mothers of one out of three firstborn children are not married at the time of conception and over half of these marry before the

99

birth of the child. And in a high proportion of cases, the marriage is unstable. Furthermore, numerous studies have clearly shown that abortion often does not have a negative emotional impact on a woman, whereas unwanted children suffer great handicaps during their development, emotionally, mentally and even physically.[2] Therefore, married or single, you are the one who has the sole right to weigh the consequences and make the decision. Your body is your own, not his.

12. YES—For the same reasons stated in the His Quiz.

13. NO—For the same reasons stated in the His Quiz.

14. NO—For the same reasons stated in the His Quiz.

15. NO—For the same reasons stated in the His Quiz.

16. NO—Gender-role liberation applies to the male as well as the female. Therefore a man should not be committed to earning as much money as possible so that his family can enjoy "the better things in life." He has the inalienable right, just as you do, to choose the kind of work he finds most self-fulfilling.

Now that you've tested your preparedness for making a marital commitment, we're ready to examine available marital choices, some of the common problems involved—regardless of socioeconomic status—and social theorists' suggested solutions. We'll also touch upon the consequences of divorce.

SOURCE NOTES FOR CHAPTER VIII:

1. Carin Rubinstein, Phillip Shaver, and Ann Peplan, "Loneliness," *Human Nature,* February, 1979, p. 60.

2. Carol C. Nadelson, "The Emotional Impact of Abortion," from *The Woman Patient* (New York: Plenum Press, 1978), pp. 176–177.

IX
FOR BETTER
OR FOR WORSE?

We've studied the various problems specifically germane to low and upper socioeconomic marriages. There are, however, a number of problems which are common to all marriages. My emphasis has been, and will continue to be, on the *problems*. However, we must not lose sight of the fact that there are numerous compensatory positives to marriage. It can be, and is, an affirmative, life-sustaining union for many couples.

Then why our rising divorce rate? Why does marriage seem to be riddled with so many problems today? It's important to keep the reasons in mind so that you don't think it's a doomed institution. It isn't. Marriage is undergoing changes in concept for the following reasons:

(1) So much more is expected of marriage today than formerly. It's no longer just a socially accepted way of living together, a sanctioned vehicle for having children.

(2) Women's awareness of their rights in society and in marriage have added a new dimension to the union and requires accommodation and understanding on the part of husbands.

(3) The strong trend toward the belief in self-gratifica-

103

tion and self-maximization have added another dimension which can sometimes cause dissension.

(4) The atmosphere of impermanence and undercurrents of turbulence in our economic and social structure are subjecting marriage to new stresses.

(5) Because marriage is being so closely scrutinized—dissected, vivisected—by social theorists to discover its structural and conceptual weaknesses, its positive facets are sometimes buried beneath the welter of negative findings.

A number of social scientists concerned about the increasing problems and high incidence of divorce have suggested marital alternatives. Their avowed purpose is to accommodate marriage to the new demands and stresses being placed upon it. The merits of these proposals have not been proven, as few of them have yet been put into actual practice. But some of the alternatives are worth noting for their constructive aspects, and, in some instances, for their impractical ones.

The Two-Tier Marriage

Tier one: A young couple foregoes the custom of becoming engaged. Instead, they get married by civil and, if desired, religious ceremony as well. But after they have been pronounced "man and wife," they do not live together. Instead, the bride continues to live with her family and the groom with his. Only after a trial period would they enter tier two and live together. This two-tier marriage is envisioned for couples in their latter teens. Supposedly, it would give them time to test their maturity and acquire a greater sense of responsibility. In addition, it would enable them to enter the final step with more financial security as it would allow them time to complete their education and to secure jobs. Among the doubtful aspects of this proposal is the assumption that contraception would be practiced and would be 100 percent effective. An even more impractical assumption is that until they entered tier two they would abstain from "Going all the way."

104

The Renewable Contract Marriage

This alternative is based upon the premise that our current marriage contract is totally unrealistic. Because it is supposed to be a lifetime commitment, it does not take into consideration existential variables. A husband or wife, or both, may undergo a change in their attitudes toward themselves, in life goals and life-style desires. Then, too, cultural and/or economic circumstances may change their attitudes toward each other. In order to accommodate marriage to these distinct possibilities, the marriage contract would have a termination date to be agreed upon prior to marriage. For example, it would automatically expire after a two-year period. It could then be renewed. A six-month advance notice of termination would be mandatory. This alternative attempts to customize the contract to the specific requirements of the couple; it is tailored to suit the desires and potentials for change and growth. This is in direct contrast to the rigidity of our present marital contract.

Trial Marriage

This alternative is nothing more nor less than living together, but with the explicit understanding that the couple intend marrying after their relationship has successfully passed the test of time and circumstances. This might have theoretical appeal, but there are too many variables to make it practical. If the couple should have a child, they might feel socially obligated to get married even if their relationship was not measuring up to expectations. Or, even if their living together were compatible, upon marriage the abrupt change to socially and legally stamped commitment might prove disruptive.

Two-Step Marriage

The great anthropologist Margaret Mead suggested this alternative. Step one is called *individual marriage,* and step two is *parental marriage*. The former takes into consideration the human need for an intimate relationship—sexual, emo-

105

tional, and intellectual. Step two ensues when and if the couple wish to have a child; thus it's termed *parental marriage*. But in order to embark on step two the couple would have to show evidence of the maturity and stability of their marriage based upon their step one relationship. In addition, they would have to offer proof to the panel of marital experts of their financial ability to support a child. It is very doubtful that Margaret Mead's proposal would ever receive legislative approval and, furthermore, the forces of tradition and religious beliefs would stand in the way of its acceptance. Then, too, minority people might look upon step two, with its conditions and economic restrictions, as elitist-mandated "genocide" permitting only the well-to-do (generally whites) to have children.

Group Marriage

This concept proposes that two or more couples live together as an extended family commune. Every facet of life would be shared: the economic, emotional, and cultural factors as well as sexual involvements. The proponents of this alternative maintain that it would have these distinct advantages: a high degree of sexual variety, a broadening and enhancing love relationship between the adults as well as for the children, whose emotional security would not depend solely on their parents. The pooling of earnings and work would offer economic advantages. These assumptions are based on the shakiest of premises: the innate stability and "goodness" of human beings. In reality there will be those who will not do their share of work; there will be individuals who may seethe with jealousy and not be able to tolerate communal sex or love. In addition, cultural values may change for some and could cause dissension.

Open Marriage

Nena and George O'Neill, in their book *Open Marriage,* proposed that a "good" marriage can be achieved if the relationship is based upon maximizing the growth potential of each partner as contrasted to the "closed" characteristics of conventional marriage. Open marriage guidelines consist of: respect for individual privacy, role flexibility, open and honest communication, equality, and trust. It also includes openness to, and acceptance of, outside contacts, both sexual and intellectual. In addition, it requires the commitment of both spouses to their own and the other's psychological needs and growth.

At first glance, open marriage may seem ideal, and so it is—ideal rather than realistic. It romanticizes marriage by defining a "good" marriage as one in which there are only positive feelings, and by claiming that negative undertones can always be resolved by open communication. It also assumes that conflicts can be resolved through give and take on each mate's part. Marital problems are assumed to be the result of unresolved neurotic tendencies and once these are eradicated—supposedly an easy matter—the "good" marriage is practically guaranteed. Unfortunately, such assumptions completely disregard social and economic stresses which greatly affect the couple. Open marriage assumes that a married couple, through the soundness of their relationship, is immune to the "warfare" of the outside world. As you've learned, this is completely unrealistic.

Since none of these marriage alternatives seems to offer *the* solution, what can you expect from marriage? To accept it as it is in the context of our culture; to regard it as an institution, or custom, which contains the potentials for an affirmative, life-sustaining relationship even though it has no lifetime warranty.

Despite our sexual freedom and the growing acceptance of couples living together, for most men and women there seems to be a psychological difference between living together and getting married. The latter has the stamp of both a public and legal commitment. The couple may be fully aware that these bonds can be severed, but being married seems to promote a greater sense of responsibility and security than just living together. Nena O'Neill, in her recent book *The Marriage Premise,* describes the phenomenon as follows:

> Ginny and Hal had been living together for four years and then decided on the spur of the moment to get married. For all their beliefs in open and free relationships, when they made the public commitment, something happened.
>   . . . Not only does the ceremony have the force of tradition behind it and the weight of history contained in its words, it is also our personal acknowledgement that we are passing into a different state in life. . . . the desire for stability and security, the recognition of our needs for belonging and for being rooted in the constancy of another's affection are everywhere, running like a thread through everyone's story. Marriage can still provide that—and something more.[1]

Aside from the O'Neills, many other social theorists believe that the viability and durability of a marriage depend upon the quality of communication between the couple. Where they are able to resolve their problems by talking them over frankly and intelligently, the prognosis for the relationship is bound to be good. Communication is an important factor, for where there is none, the gap will create a chasm. But communication, per se, is studded with barbs.

For a couple to live together harmoniously requires certain rules: rules as to the kind of work each will engage in, the degree of involvement each should have in the other's work; rules governing household chore responsibilities, the roles outsiders, including in-laws, play in the marriage. Communication can do a good deal to resolve such problems. But who establishes the rules for making the rules? This is how one social scientist describes the problems arising from communication as it pertains to marital sex:

. . . sex is supposed to be the ultimate refuge from the rat race, but achievement pressures exist as much in the bedroom as elsewhere. On the one hand, sex is supposed to be a free surrender to basic impulses and instincts; on the other hand, what you do and when you do it are supposed to be in tune with the needs of the other person. Each partner is supposed to let the other know what he or she wants. If a person doesn't communicate this information, he/she may be frustrated and this frustration may spoil the partner's pleasure directly or indirectly. But the horn of the dilemma is this: if one person communicates his/her own needs too clearly or too insistently, then the partner is likely to resent being *told* what to do; he/she may feel like a masturbatory tool of the other person rather than a free sexual being.[2]

Thus open communication is not the entire answer. Furthermore, the majority of studies of marriage are based on the assumption that a marriage is either "good" or "bad." This sounds reasonable enough. But what constitutes a "good" or "bad" marriage? The guidelines established by many social scientists for making the distinction often tend to be unrealistic and arbitrary. And their conclusions are based mainly upon studies of couples whose marriages are either on the brink of dissolution or have been terminated.

However, one team of social scientists, for their study, chose 437 successful, "normal" couples. They ranged in age from thirty-five to fifty-five, had stable marriages, and were in the top income bracket. These researchers made the interesting discovery that "good" marriages, within a group of people of similar social status, vary enormously in kinds of relationships. They found that, instead of there being just one kind of "good" marriage, there were five different kinds of good, enduring marriages. They were catalogued as follows:

The *Conflict-Habituated Marriage*. In the conflict-loaded marriage the husband and wife fight with one another continually. Just being together starts an argument, and they engage in their verbal battles in front of their family just as freely as in private. But they do not consider this a cause for divorce. Quite the contrary, they define their verbal duels as acceptable means of communicating with each other. The investigators concluded that husband and wife are filled with a great deal of hostility which must have an outlet, and that their battles serve to bind them together.

The Devitalized Marriage. The term "devitalized" does not apply to the individuals themselves, but to their relationship. Their marriage starts off on a romantic basis with a show of love and closeness. But over the years they drift apart. Nevertheless, they get along together and have no inclination or desire to sever their limited relationship.

The Passive-Congenial Marriage. In contrast to the devitalized marriage, the couples involved in this one were never highly emotionally charged with each other at the outset. It can be described as a "cool" kind of relationship of mutual convenience. It allows husband and wife to devote their creative energies and interests outside the home. They feel that the stereotype romantic marriage is self-limiting, and theirs is the way a marriage ought to be—at least for them.

The Vital Marriage. It approaches the conventional concept of a "good" marriage. The term "vital" refers to the quality of the relationship, not to the makeup of the individuals. In this marriage, the couple enjoy being with each other and spend a lot of time sharing experiences and activities together. This closeness, however, does not make the partners feel that they are losing their self-identity.

The Total Marriage. This is a variation on the vital marriage and carries togetherness one step closer. Husband and wife share even more experiences and interests together. She, for example, involves herself in numerous ways in her husband's work. They state that their marriage style is frequently criticized by other couples who either doubt that it's as good as it seems or feel that the couple must be immature to depend on each other to such an extent.

This study and its conclusions are by no means definitive, and its investigators do not claim that it is. Other researchers might have arrived at different conclusions, and a study of lower socioeconomic couples might reveal different findings.

Studies have been made of marriages over a protracted period of time, from engagement until fifteen to twenty years later. Some have shown that certain areas in the relationship decline. They include demonstrable affection and sex. Other studies have shown that many marriages improve with time. Many books come off the press each year purporting to show how to achieve marital happiness. Some may be helpful; others are arcane and dogmatic. All the studies and all the books combined cannot solve the riddle of marriage, because marriage, like life, includes an almost endless list of variables. They cover the gamut: the emotional makeup of each of the partners, the effects of their childhood experiences, their genetic makeup, their reactions to social and economic stresses. It's an almost limitless assortment of circumstances to which each may react differently.

Considering this welter of confusion, how can you evaluate the prospect of marriage constructively? It is hoped, by having a heightened awareness of the more common causes of marital unhappiness. These "common problems" are based upon studies made by social theorists and their conclusions are not guaranteed to be 100 percent objective. But the study I have selected seems to offer helpful and sensible observations. It compartmentalizes the problem into eight categories:

Affectional Problems. Signs of affection and love are sometimes subject to attrition. This is often due to the high demands placed upon modern marriage. When they are not met, disillusionment and disappointment ensue. In earlier times less was expected of the union. Women's expectations, especially, were far more limited. Companionship, shared cul-

111

tural interests, and equal pleasure from sex were not part of her marital happiness package. Another cause for affectional deterioration can be today's belief in self-maximization and self-fulfillment—narcissism.

How can a couple resolve such problems? By becoming aware that their expectations may have been too high, that they need to be tailored to functional size. Furthermore, a partner should realize that self-maximization must come from self, but not at the expense of the other.

Sexual Problems. Sexual difficulties can seriously mar the relationship. If they stem from deep-seated emotional hang-ups on either mates' or both mates' part, the solution can be difficult. Psychotherapy, if the therapist is proficient, or sex clinics, if affordable, may offer the only solution.

However, sexual incompatibility may arise from the expectations which liberated women have from sexual union. These have already been described previously (see pages 84–86). Solution? The male will have to learn to adjust with the aid of his mate.

Personality Problems. Living together under one roof; sharing bedroom, bath, kitchen, friends, and meshing life-styles requires a lot of adjustment. Each partner brings to marriage habit patterns which he and she acquired in the past. They can be the cause of irritation and dissension. They often resemble an opened Pandora's Box. Some examples are: lack of personal hygiene, untidiness, irritating social manners which cause embarrassment, a dramatic display of moodiness to achieve attention. A couple must be aware that marriage requires compromise linked with mutual consideration.

Role-Task Problems. Generally these arise from sex-role stereotyping: Males and females are biologically programmed to perform specific tasks. Women are expected to do household chores and child tending, while men are the economic providers. As you've already learned, society, not nature, assigned these roles. Also, they do not reflect the reality of most married couples' situation. Many young husbands and wives without children have jobs. Consequently, household chores should be shared equally. Furthermore, more and more wives with children are working, either from economic necessity or because they find housework self-limiting (see page 96, where we discussed the resolution of this problem).

Parental-Role Problems. While the prospect of parenthood for teen-agers may seem remote, this is not the case. About 10 percent of all women under twenty become pregnant each year and about two-thirds of these approximately six hundred thousand pregnancies are unintended.[4] Therefore the problems arising from young parenthood require some discussion.

Women under twenty are least prepared emotionally for pregnancy, childbearing, and child rearing. Furthermore, ensuing monetary stress can be a source of trouble. Family income is cut because the wife cannot work for a period of time, nor can three live as cheaply as two. Numerous emotional problems crop up as well, especially if the young couple's prime motive for marrying was the unwanted pregnancy. Because of the emotional immaturity of both parents, the infant is more apt to rupture rather than bind the relationship. The father may resent the time and attention his wife devotes to the child and feel neglected. This is also apt to occur with older couples. The mother, on her part, may resent that the husband does not share in parental chores such as diaper changing and baby tending. Eventually, disagreements may arise on how to rear the child. Parenthood, unlike marriage, *is* a lifetime commitment and should not be entered into lightly or accidentally. As Planned Parenthood suggests: Love carefully.

Intercultural Problems. They can arise from differences in religious beliefs and from a couple's relationship with parents and in-laws. Disagreements over religious principles should have been resolved prior to marriage (see page 96). If such is not the case, marital counseling would be in order. If there is a loving relationship, in all likelihood these problems can be resolved.

113

Problems arising from relationships with parents and in-laws are far more difficult to resolve. An emotionally mature person will have ceased to be dependent on parents. If either husband or wife has not severed the umbilical cord, this can cause fundamental problems. Interference in life-styles by in-laws can be another source of trouble. If a couple is financially dependent on their in-laws, they can alter the situation by cutting the golden cord. If they are not financially beholden and have a solidly based relationship with each other, firm refusal of parental interference, though difficult, is the only recourse.

Deviant Behavior Problems. The term "deviant" applies to behavior markedly different from approved norms. It encompasses compulsive gambling, excessive drinking (far too common), and extramarital sex. Compulsive gambling and alcoholism, especially, are difficult and, in most instances, impossible to cure. If cure appears impossible, divorce is the only solution if the well partner wants to survive. The problem of extramarital sex has many ramifications and causes as well as possible solutions which have been covered previously (see pages 97–98).

Situational Condition Problems. These arise from circumstances beyond the couple's control: financial difficulties and ill health. You have already seen that serious monetary woes create marital woes even where the marriage is well grounded. There is no guaranteed solution except to acquire more money. Deplorable housing conditions, inadequate diet and medical care and the resulting emotional chaos will be resolved only when our entire social structure undergoes a drastic change.

Coping with one's mate's ill health is part of the commitment which each has made—not because the marriage vow states "in sickness and in health," but because a loving, close relationship transcends the situation and does not allow sickness to erode it.

We've reached the end of our survey of marital problems,

114

possible solutions, conditions and circumstances. We've studied the twirling of the marry-go-round from prehistoric times through today. We've learned that, for better or for worse, it's kept spinning, in one form or another, for hundreds of thousands of years.

Because of the drastic changes in our social structure—from a hunting and gathering society to today's nuclear-industrial one—the original purpose of marriage, economic and life-supportive, has spun off the marry-go-round. The extended family of the agricultural era has given way to the nuclear family. Properly educated and vocationally equipped, a woman can make it on her own financially. This has changed the husband's familial role from that of sole breadwinner and family head to that of partner in the union. Because of the advances in contraception, to be or not to be a parent is within our control. This is one of the reasons why an increasing number of women are becoming aware that their human potential is no longer limited to motherhood. They gradually are approaching equal status in our social structure. Men, in turn, gradually are learning how to live without their papier-mâché macho armor—fearlessness, emotionlessness, aggressiveness, and pseudosexual prowess.

The institution of marriage is very much alive, though not so well. It's alive because of the human need for companionship, for wanting to love and be loved, because of the increasing need for emotional support and, of course, for sexual enjoyment. Being married gives these hoped-for benefits the seal of security and commitment for which there seems to be no other substitute. Marriage is not so well because of the very demands made upon it. But our high divorce rate is not necessarily proof of its failure. Perhaps instead it is because men and women feel that they have the right to at least search for greater self-development and maximization of their individual human potential.

I stated at the outset that the purpose of this book was to provide you with an overview and insight into marriage as it really is today and what it can mean for you tomorrow. Marriage is no longer a social "must," but an alternative. More people are remaining single than ever before, and others are opting for homosexual relationships.

However, since the great majority continue to prefer marriage, for all the good reasons we have described, it should be entered into not guardedly but wisely—certainly not as an escape from loneliness, but as an affirmation of a loving relationship. It should not be looked upon as a guarantee of lifetime bliss, but as a shared, enriching experience that is subject both to human frailties and to social stresses beyond one's control.

Therefore it is vital that you take a long, hard look at yourself and your intended partner before you leap into the marriage bed. Carefully scrutinize yourself and your partner-to-be, your motives for wanting to get married, the solidity of the relationship you have established with one another. And because of the role which money, not just love, plays in matrimony, you have to take financial ability into account as well. Above all, don't look upon the prospect of marriage as your life goal. That is self-limiting. Marriage should be regarded as a means to an end. The end is to transform the mundane business of being into an act of affirmation. If entered into maturely and knowledgeably, marriage can play a great part in achieving that affirmation.

SOURCE NOTES FOR CHAPTER IX:

1. Nena O'Neill, *The Marriage Premise* (New York: M. Evans Co., 1977), pp. 29–30.
2. Skolnik, *The Intimate Environment,* p. 255.
3. Ibid., pp. 264–265.
4. Malkah T. Notman and Carol C. Nadelson, eds., *The Woman Patient* (New York: Plenum Press, 1978), p. 210.

INDEX

Affectional problem, 111–112

Blacks, 69–70

Communication, 108–109
Conflict-habituated marriage, 110
Contract marriage, 105

Deviant behavior, 114
Devitalized marriage, 110

Economic angst, 62–63
Economic stresses, 42
Extramarital sex, 39

Family structure
    agricultural revolution, 15–20

factors of, 5–8
hunting and gathering societies, 4, 13–15
Industrial Revolution, 20–22
mid-nineteenth century to mid-twentieth century, 25–32
Fromm, Erich, 6–7, 82

Gender-role stereotyping, 48–49, 50, 75–78
Group marriage, 106

Health stresses, 42
Hunting and gathering societies, 4, 13–15
Husband, family role, 6

Intercultural problems, 113–114

117

Job anguish, 63–65

Leisure activities, 14–15
Living together, 107
Love, 49–50, 78–83

Marital alternatives, 104–107
Marital preparedness quizzes, 89–100
Marital unhappiness, causes of, 111–114
Mead, Margaret, 105–106
Middle class, 36–37, 47–55

O'Neill, George, 106–107
O'Neill, Nena, 106–107, 108
Open marriage, 106–107
Ovid, 78–79

Parental-role problems, 113
Partner selection, external forces on, 48
Passive-congenial marriage, 110
Personality problems, 112
Premarital quizzes, 89–100
Protestant work ethic, 37–38
Puritanism, 16–19

Renewable contract marriage, 105
Role-task problems, 112–113

Romantic love, 80

Self, 38, 50
Sex-role stereotyping, 48–49, 50, 75–78
Sexual adjustment, 41–42
Sexual problems, 112
Sexuality, 83–86, 108–109
Situational condition problems, 114
Social stresses, 41–43
Society, changes in, 4–8, 13–22
Socioeconomic class, 35–43
    middle class, 36–37, 47–55
    working class, 36, 59–70

Total marriage, 110–111
Trial marriage, 105
Two-step marriage, 105–106
Two-tier marriage, 104

Unemployment, 37, 64, 69–70

Values, conflicting, 6–7
Vital marriage, 110

Wife, role in the family, 5–6
Women's liberation, 42–43
Working class, 36, 59–70